E. A

MW01088140

Studies in
Christian Education

"Now, as never before, we need to understand the true science of education. If we fail to understand this, we shall never have a place in the kingdom of God."

Ellen G. White, *Christian Educator*, August 1, 1897.

Adventist Pioneer Library

37457 Jasper Lowell Rd
Jasper, OR, 97438, USA
+1 (877) 585-1111
www.APLib.org

Originally published in 1915 and republished in 1952 for classes at the Madison School.

Published in the USA

June, 2016

ISBN: 978-1-61455-034-1

STUDIES IN CHRISTIAN EDUCATION

Education Experiences Before the

Midnight Cry

compared with

Education Experiences Before the

Loud Cry

"Now as never before we need to understand the true science of education. If we fail to understand this we shall never have a place in the Kingdom of God."

Ellen G. White, *Christian Educator*, August 1, 1897

E. A. Sutherland

EDWARD ALEXANDER SUTHERLAND (1865-1955)

CONTENTS

FOREWORD TO THE 2015 EDITION

✦✦✦

It has given me a thrill and much satisfaction knowing that others in a different part of the world and a very different era in time, may find challenge, instruction, and good Christian camaraderie, from the following book, written by my grandfather, Edward Alexander Sutherland.

I grew up always standing a little bit taller, feeling in the wake of God's stanch people, happy to be a granddaughter of E. A. Sutherland. Early on I knew he had gone back to school to take medicine "at forty years old," while continuing to direct the school at Madison. Also, that he and Percy Magan had done this together, commuting on motorcycles!

His life was in Madison, Tennessee, whereas, I lived in Pasadena, California. At our house he was referred to as E. A. by all but my Mother, Yolanda Sutherland Brunie, who would refer to him as "my Father." We did not travel much during the war (World War II). But there were some calls back and forth by telephone, and E. A. and the Madison school were always part of our reality. My earliest recollections of actually being with him was when he and my grandmother, Sally Brailier Sutherland, visited us out here after the war. Later, my Mother and I drove to spend a week there in Tennessee with her family, staying at her brother's farm, my Uncle Joe's place near Madison. By then, my grandfather, Dr. E. A., also lived there with Joe and his family.

By that time, July 1952, I was half way through college at La Sierra (now La Sierra University), and was much more interested to sit for extended discussions with E. A. on Bible passages, on his attitudes toward multiple areas, and definitely on how it was that Ellen White had been important in deciding on the property there at Madison to build a school. E. A. "marked me" with his passion for pursuing goodness, his energy for investing in living in the present moment, and his strong, friendly, warm presence.

I am very grateful for the persons living since that time who have kept many of our founding leaders present to us through their historic writing.

Blessing to those using this book.

Barbara Brunie Jones

May, 2015

ORIGINAL FOREWORD

The Students' Volunteer Band, studying fields of missionary activity in the Nashville Agricultural and Normal Institute, had the privilege of attending a series of studies given by Dr. E. A. Sutherland, president of the institution, revealing the fact that the great Protestant denominations failed to give the first angel's message in its fullness because they did not free themselves from the papal system of education. Clinging to this system in the end brought them into confusion.

The Seventh-day Adventist denomination came into existence because of this failure, and it must succeed where the others failed. Their birthright as a denomination is a great reform movement, the greatest the world has ever known. The Lord has been telling our people that, as individuals, we are in a positive danger of suffering the same defeat as they suffered, because we still cling to worldly methods of education. They failed to give the midnight cry because of their wrong system of education. We are soon to enter the period of the latter rain. We trust the following pages may be earnestly and prayerfully read.

1. Beginning of the Educational History in the United States

That church triumphs which breaks the yoke of worldly education, and which develops and practices the principles of Christian education.

> "Now, as never before, we need to understand the true science of education. If we fail to understand this we shall never have a place in the kingdom of God." (Ellen G. White, *Christian Educator*, August 1, 1897).

> "The science of true education is the truth. … The third angel's message is truth." (Ellen G. White, *Testimonies for the Church*, Vol. 6, p. 131).

It is taken for granted that all Seventh-day Adventists believe that Christian education and the third angel's message are the same truth. The two are as inseparable as are a tree's roots and its trunk and branches.

The object of these studies is to give a better understanding of the reason for the decline and moral fall of the Protestant denominations at the time of the midnight cry in 1844, and to help us as Seventh-day Adventists to avoid their mistakes as we approach the loud cry, soon due to the world.

A brief survey of the history of the Protestant denominations shows that their spiritual downfall in 1844 was the result of their failure "to understand the true science of education." Their failure to understand and to practice Christian education unfitted them to proclaim to the world the message of Christ's second coming. The Seventh-day Adventist denomination was then called into existence to take up the work which the popular churches had failed to train their missionaries to do. The Protestant denomination could not give the third angel's message, a reform movement, which is a warning against the beast and his image, because they were still clinging to those doctrines and those principles of education which themselves form the beast and his image. It is important that young Seventh-day Adventists study seriously the causes of the spiritual decline of these churches in 1844, lest we repeat their history, and be cast aside the Spirit of God, and thus lose our place in the kingdom. If Seventh-day Adventist succeed where they failed, we must have a system of education which repudiates those principles which in themselves develop the beast and his image. "Now, all these things happened unto them for ensamples; and they are written for our admonition upon whom the ends of the world are come."

Protestantism, born in the sixteenth century, was about to lose its light in Europe. God then prepared a new land, the future United States, as a cradle for the protection and development of those principles, and from this country is to go forth the final world-wide message that heralds the Savior's return.

> "It was a desire for liberty of conscience that inspired the Pilgrims to brave the perils of the long journey across the sea, to endure the hardships and dangers of the wilderness, and, with God's blessing, to lay on the shores of America the foundation of a mighty nation... The Bible was held as the foundation of faith, and source of wisdom and the charter of liberty. Its principles were diligently taught in the home, in the school and in the church, and its fruits were manifest in thrift, intelligence, purity and temperance... It was demonstrated that the principles of the Bible are the surest safeguards to national greatness." (Ellen G. White, *Great Controversy*, pp. 292, 296).

These reformers, on reaching America, renounced the Papal doctrines in church and state, but they retained the Papal system of education.

> "While the reformers rejected the creed of Rome, they were not entirely free from her spirit of intolerance. ... The English reformers, while renouncing the doctrines of Romanism, had retained many of its forms. ... [Some] looked upon them as badges of the slavery from which they had been delivered, and to which they had no disposition to return. ... Many earnestly desired to return to the purity and simplicity which characterized the primitive church... 'England was ceasing forever to be a habitable place.' Some at last determined to seek refuge in Holland. Difficulties, losses and imprisonment were encountered. ... In their flight they had left their houses, their goods, their means of livelihood... They cheerfully accepted the situation, and lost no time in idleness or repining. ... 'They knew they were pilgrims'. ... In the midst of exile and hardship their love and faith waxed strong. They trusted the Lord's promises, and He did not fail them in time of need. ... And when God's hand seemed pointing them across the sea, to a land where they might found for themselves a state and leave to their children the precious heritage of religious

liberty, they went forward without shrinking, in the path of Providence. ... The Puritans had joined themselves together by a solemn covenant as the Lord's free people, 'to walk together in all His ways made known or to be made known to them.' Here was the true spirit of reform, the vital principle of Protestantism." (*Ibid.*, pp. 289, 293).

The educational system of the church, which had driven them from their native home, was one of the most serious errors from which the Puritans failed to break away. This system of education, while Papal in spirit, was, to a certain extent, Protestant in form. The historian writes of the schools of the Puritans in the New World, that their courses were

> "fitted to the time-sanctioned curriculum of the college. They taught much Latin and Greek, an extended course in mathematics, and were strong generally on the side of the humanities... This was a modeling after Rugby Eton and other noted English schools." (Richard G. Boone, *Education in the United States*, p. 71 [1889]).

Again we read, "The roots of this system were deep in the great ecclesiastical system." "From his early training," Dunster, one of the first presidents of Harvard, "patterned the Harvard course largely after that of the English Universities." They so faithfully patterned after the English model—Cambridge University—that they were called by that name, and the historian wrote of Harvard, "In several instances youths in the parent country were sent to the American Cambridge for a finishing education." Boone, speaking of the courses of study of William and Mary prior to the Revolution, says, "All were of English pattern." Of Yale, started later, it is said, "The regulations for the most part were those at Harvard, as also the courses of study." The younger patterned after the older. It is very natural that Yale should be established after the English Papal system, because the founder, Elihu Yale, had spent twenty years in the English schools. "Twenty years he spent in the schools and in special study." (*Ibid.*, pp. 24-40).

Seventh-day Adventists should not let this fact escape their attention: the three leading schools of the colonies were established by men who had fled from the Papal doctrines of the Old World; but these educators, because of their training in these Papal schools and their ignorance of the relation between education and religion, unwittingly patterned their institutions after the educational system of the church from which they had withdrawn. It is surprising that these English Reformers, after sacrificing as they did for a worthy cause, should yet allow a system of education, so unfitted to all their purposes, to be in reality the nurse of their children, from whose bosom these children drew their nourishment. They did not realize that the character and Christian experience of these children depended upon the nature of the food received. Had they grasped the relation of the education of the child to the experience of the same individual in the church, they would not have borrowed this Papal system of education, but would have cast it out bodily as too dangerous for tolerance within the limits of Protestantism.

Some facts from educational history will make clear the statement that the system of education in Oxford, Cambridge, Eton and Rugby was Papal, and the New England reformers, patterning their schools after these models, were planting the Papal system of education in America. Laurie says, "Oxford and Cambridge modeled themselves largely after Paris... A large number of masters and their pupils left Paris... Thus the English portion of (Paris) University went to Oxford and Cambridge." The relation of the University of Paris, the mother of Cambridge and Oxford, to the Papacy is thus expressed, "It was because it was the center of theological learning that it received so many privileges from the Pope, and was kept in close relation to the Papal See." (Simon S. Laurie, *The Rise and Early Constitution of Universities*, pp. 153, 162, 242).

Luther and Melanchthon, the great sixteenth century reformers, understood clearly that it was impossible to have a permanent religious reform without Christian education. So they not only gave attention to the doctrines of the Papacy, but also developed a strong system of Christian schools. Melanchthon said, "To neglect the young in our schools is just like taking the spring out of the year. They indeed take away the spring from the year who permit the schools to decline, because religion cannot be maintained without them." "Melanchthon steadily directed his efforts to the advancement of education and the building up of good Christian schools... In the spring of 1525, with Luther's help, he reorganized the schools of Eisleben and Madgeburg." He declared, "The cause of true education is the cause of God." (Joseph Stump, *Life of Philipe Melanchton*, p. 81).

"In 1528 Melanchthon drew up the 'Saxony School Plan,' which served as the basis of organization for many schools throughout Germany." This plan dealt with the question of a "multiplicity of studies that were not only unfruitful but even hurtful. ... The teacher should not burden the children with too many books." (F. V. N. Painter, *A History of Education*, p. 152). These reformers realized that the strength of the Papal church lay in its educational system, and they struck a crushing blow at this system and, wounding it, brought the Papal church to her knees. The reformers established a system of Christian schools that made Protestants of the children. This wonderful revolution in education and religion was accomplished in one generation, in the brief space of one man's life.

To give an idea of the power in that great Christian educational movement, the historian, speaking of several European countries, says:

> "The nobility of that country studied in Wittenberg—all the colleges of the land were filled with Protestants... Not more than the thirtieth part of the population remained Catholic... They withheld their children, too, from the [Catholic] schools. ... The inhabitants of Mainz too did not hesitate to send their children to Protestant schools. ... The Protestant notions extended their vivifying energies to the most remote and most forgotten corners of Europe. What an immense domain had they conquered within the space of forty years. ... Twenty years had elapsed in Vienna since a single student of the University had taken priests' orders... About this period the teachers in Germany were all, almost without exceptions, Protestants. The whole body of the rising generation sat at their feet and imbibed a hatred of the Pope with the first rudiments of learning" (Leopold Von Ranke, *History of the Popes, Their Church and State, in the Sixteenth and Seventeenth Centuries*, 1844, p. 164-167).

After the death of Luther and Melanchthon, the theologians, into whose hands the work of the Reformation fell, instead of multiplying Christian schools, became absorbed in the mere technicalities of theology, and passed by the greatest work of the age. They sold their birthright for a mess of pottage. When the successors of Luther and Melanchthon failed to continue that constructive work, which centered largely in the education of the youth, who were to be the future missionaries and pillars of the church, internal dissension arose. Their time was spent very largely in criticizing the views of some of their colaborers who differed with them on some unimportant points of theology. Thus they became destructive instead of constructive. They paid much attention to doctrines, and spent the most of their energy in preserving orthodoxy. They crystallized their doctrines into a creed; they ceased to develop, and lost the spirit of Christian education, which was the oil for their lamps. Protestantism degenerated into dead orthodoxy, and they broke up into opposing factions. The Protestant church, thus weakened, could not resist the great power of rejuvenated Papal education.

The success of the reformers had been due to their control of the young people through their educational system. The Papal schools were almost forsaken during the activity of Luther and Melanchthon. But when these reformers died and their successors became more interested in abstract theology than in Christian education, and spent their time, energy and the money of the church in preaching and writing on abstract theology, the Papal school system, recovering itself, rose to a life and death struggle with the Protestant church. The Papacy realized that the existence of the Papal church itself depended upon a victory over Protestant schools. We are surprised at the skill and tact the Papal educators used in their attack, and the rapidity with which they gained the victory. This experience should be an object lesson forever to Seventh-day Adventists.

A christian school animated by the papal spirit.—The eyes of the successors of Luther and Melanchthon were blinded. They did not understand "the true science of education." They did not see its importance, and grasp the dependence of character upon education. "The true object of education is to restore the image of God in the soul." (*Christian Education*, p. 63). Satan took advantage of this blindness to cause some of their own educators, like wolves in sheep's clothing, to prey on the lambs. Chief among these was John Sturm, who, by these blind reformers, was supposed to be a good Protestant. Sturm introduced practically the entire Papal system of education into the Protestant schools of Strasburg. And because he pretended to be a Protestant, the successors of Luther looked with favor upon his whole educational scheme. He was regarded by the so-called reformers as the greatest educator of his time, and his school became so popular among Protestants that it was taken as their model for the Protestant schools of Germany, and its "influence extended to England, and thence to America. ... 'No one who is acquainted with the education given at our principal classical schools, Eton, Winchester and Westminster, forty years ago, can fail to see that their curriculum was framed in a great degree on Sturm's model.'" The historian says that it was Sturm's ambition "to reproduce Greece and Rome in the midst of modern Christian civilization." (*A History of Education*, p. 162).

This educational wolf, dressed in a Christian fleece, made great inroads on the lambs of the flock, and made possible a Papal victory. Most dangerous of all enemies in a church is a school of its own, Christian in profession, with "teachers and managers who are only half converted"; who are "accustomed to popular methods"; who "concede some things and make half reforms; ... preferring to work according to their own ideas" (*Testimonies for the Church*, Vol. 6, p. 141), who, step by step, advance toward worldly education leading the innocent lambs with them. In the day of judgment it will be easier for that man who has been cold and an avowed enemy to a reform movement than for that one who professes to be a shepherd, but who has been a wolf in sheep's clothing, who deceives the lambs until they are unable to save themselves. It is the devil's master stroke for the overthrow of God's work in the world, and there is no influence harder to counteract. No other form of evil is so strongly denounced. "I know why works that thou are neither cold nor hot. I would that thou wert cold or hot. So then because thou art lukewarm and neither cold or hot, I will spue thee out of my mouth." (Revelation 3:15, 16).

Sturm's school stood as a half-way mark between the Christian schools of Luther and Melanchthon and the Papal schools round about him. It offered a mixture of mediaeval, classical literature with a thin slice of Scripture, sandwiched in for effect, and flavored with the doctrines of the church. Its course of study was impractical; its methods of instruction mechanical; memory work was exalted; its government was arbitrary and empirical.

> "A dead knowledge of words took the place of a living knowledge of things. ... The pupils were obliged to learn, but they were not educated to see and hear, to think and prove, and were not led to a true independence and personal perfection; the teachers found their function

in teaching the prescribed text, not in harmoniously developing the young human being according to the laws of Nature." (*A History of Education*, p. 156-157).

Macaulay, speaking of this system of education, adds:

"They promised what was impracticable; they despised what was practicable; they filled the world with long words and long beards; and they left it as wicked and as ignorant as they found it." (Thomas B. Macaulay, "Lord Bacon", *Critical and Historical Essays Contributed to the Edinburgh Review*, Vol. 2, 1877, p. 389).

Jesuit schools.—This study should make it clear that the Protestant teachers weakened and unfitted the Protestant denomination for the attack made by the Papacy through the counter system of education introduced by Loyola, founder of the order of Jesuits. Before this the Catholic church realized its helplessness to withstand the great movement of Protestantism, inaugurated by thousands of missionaries trained in the Christian schools of Luther and Melanchthon. Noting the return of the Protestant church to dead orthodoxy under the inefficient leadership of Luther's successors, the Papacy recognized the vulnerable point in Protestantism.

The order of Jesuits found its special mission in combating the Reformation. As the most effective means of arresting the progress of Protestantism, it aimed at controlling education. "It developed an immense educational activity" in Protestant countries,

"and earned for its schools a great reputation... More than any other agency it stayed the progress of the Reformation, and it even succeeded in winning back territory already conquered by Protestantism. ... It worked chiefly through its schools, of which it established and controlled large numbers. ... Every member of the order became a competent and practical teacher." (*A History of Education*, p. 167-169).

The following methods of teaching are characteristic of Jesuit schools: "*The memory* was cultivated as a means of keeping down free activity of thought and clearness of judgment." In the place of self-government, their method of discipline was a "system of mutual distrust, espionage and informing. *Implicit obedience* relieved the pupils from all responsibility as to the moral justification of their deeds." (Karl Rosenkranz, *The Philosophy of Education*, p. 270-271).

"The Jesuits made much of emulation. ... 'He who knows how to excite emulation has found the most powerful auxiliary in his teaching. ... Nothing will be more honorable than to outstrip a fellow student, and nothing more dishonorable than to be outstripped. Prizes will be distributed to the best pupils with the greatest possible solemnity.' ... It sought showy results with which to dazzle the world. A well-rounded development was nothing. ... 'The Jesuits did not aim at developing *all* the faculties of their pupils, but merely the receptive and reproductive faculties. ... [When a student] could make a brilliant display from the resources of a well-stored memory, he had reached the highest points to which the Jesuits sought to lead him. Originality and independence of mind, love of truth for its own sake, the power of reflecting, and of forming correct judgments, were not merely neglected, they were suppressed in the Jesuits' system.'" (*A History of Education*, pp. 171-173).

"The Jesuit system of education ... was remarkably successful, and for a century nearly all the foremost men of Christendom came from Jesuit schools." (*The Philosophy of Education*, p. 271).

Success of Jesuit schools.—Concerning the success of the Jesuit educational system in overcoming the careless and indifferent Protestants, we read: "They carried their point." They shadowed the Protestant schools and, like a parasite, sucked from them their life. "Their labors were above all devoted to the Universities. ... Protestants called back their children from distant schools, and put them under the care of the Jesuits. ... [The Jesuits] occupied the professors' chairs. ... They conquered the Germans on their own soil, in their very home, and wrested from them a part of their native land." (*History of the Popes, Their Church and State*, p. 170-172). This conquest rapidly went on through nearly all European countries. They conquered England by taking English youth to Rome and educating them in Jesuit schools, and sending them back as missionaries and teachers to their native land. And thus they were established in the schools of England. The Jesuits overran the new world also, becoming thoroughly established, and have been employing their characteristic methods here ever since. Here, as elsewhere, their only purpose is "to obtain the sole direction of education, so that by getting the young into their hands they can fashion them after their own pattern." (Richard E. Thopson, *Footprints of the Jesuits*, p. 419).

"Within fifty years from the day Luther burned the Bull of Leo before the gates of Wittenberg Protestantism gained its highest ascendancy, an ascendancy which it soon lost, and which it has never regained." (Thomas B. Macaulay, "Essay on Von Ranke's History of the Popes", *The Edinburgh Review*, pp. 236, 237).

"How was it that Protestantism did so much, yet did no more? How was it that the church of Rome, having lost a large part of Europe, not only ceased to lose, but actually regained nearly half of what she had lost? This is certainly a most curious and important question." (*Ibid.*, p. 227).

We have already had the answer, but it is well stated thus by Macaulay, who understood the part played by the Jesuit schools founded by Loyola:

"Such was the celebrated Ignatius Loyola, who, in the great reaction, bore the same part which Luther bore in the great Protestant movement. It was at the feet of that Jesuit that the youth of the higher and middle classes were brought up from childhood to manhood, from the first rudiments to the courses of rhetoric and philosophy... The great order went forth conquering and to conquer... Their first object was to drive no person out of the pale of the church." (*Ibid.*, pp. 240, 241).

Heresy hunting defeats the Protestant cause:—Macaulay thus gives the causes for this defeat of Protestantism and the success of the Papacy:

"The war between Luther and Leo was a war between firm faith and unbelief; between zeal and apathy; between energy and indolence; between seriousness and frivolity; between a pure morality and vice. Very different was the war which degenerate Protestantism had to wage against regenerate Catholicism," [made possible by the Jesuit educational system]. (*Ibid.*, pp. 244, 245).

"The reformers had contracted some of the corruptions which had been justly censured in the Church of Rome. They had become lukewarm and worldly. Their great old leaders had been borne to the grave and had left no successors... Everywhere on the Protestant side we see languor; everywhere on the Catholic side we see ardor and devotion. Almost the whole zeal of the Protestants was directed against each other. Within the Catholic church there were no serious disputes on points of doctrine... On the other hand, the force which ought to have fought the battle of the Reformation was exhausted in civil conflict." (*Ibid.*, p. 245).

The papacy learned a bitter lesson in dealing with heretics. Since the Reformation she conserves her strength by setting them to work.

Macaulay says,

> "Rome thoroughly understands what no other church has ever under-
> stood—how to deal with enthusiasts... The Catholic church neither
> submits to enthusiasm nor prescribes it, but uses it... She accordingly
> enlists him (the enthusiast) in her services... For a man thus minded
> there is within the pale of the establishment (Orthodox Protestant
> churches) no place. He has been at no college; ... and he is told that if he
> remains in the communion of the church he must do so as a hearer, and
> that, if he is resolved to be teacher, he must begin by being a schismatic
> (a heretic). His choice is soon made; he harangues on Tower Hill or in
> Smithfield. A congregation is formed, and in a few weeks the (Prot-
> estant) church has lost forever a hundred families." (*Ibid.*, p. 247-249).

The Papacy was wiser than the Protestants in dealing with those
who became somewhat irregular in their views. She spent little in church
trials. She directed their efforts, instead of attempting to force them
from the church.

> "The ignorant enthusiast whom the English church makes ... a most
> dangerous enemy, the Catholic church makes a champion. She bids
> him nurse his beard, covers him with a gown and hood of coarse dark
> stuff, ties a rope about his waist, and sends him forth to teach in her
> name. He costs her nothing. He takes not a ducat away from the
> regular clergy. He lives by the alms of those who respect his spiritual
> character and are grateful for his instructions... All this influence is
> employed to strengthen the church... In this way the church of Rome
> unites in herself all the strength of the establishment (organization)
> and all the strength of dissent... Place Ignatius Loyola at Oxford. He
> is certain to become the head of a formidable secession. Place John
> Wesley at Rome. He is certain to be the first general of a new society
> devoted to the interest and honor of the church." (*Ibid.*, p. 249-250).

The church of Rome since its rejuvenation is literally alive with determined, enthusiastic, zealous soldiers who know nothing but to live, to be
spent, and to die for the church. She is determined to conquer and bring
back humiliated, broken down, and completely subjugated, the Protestant
denominations. She has everywhere, through her Jesuit teachers, editors,
and public officials, men at work to fashion public sentiment, to capture
the important and controlling positions of government and most of all, to
obtain control through her teachers of the minds of Protestant children
and youth. She values that eternal principle, and makes use of it, "Train up

a child in the way he should go, and when he is old he will not depart from it." Let me teach a child until he is twelve years old, say the Catholics, and he will always remain a Catholic. We can now better comprehend why those English reformers did not understand the character and the danger of the school system in vogue at Cambridge, Oxford, Eton, and Westminster, and unwittingly planted this system of education upon the shores of their new home and in every one of their Christian schools. They ignorantly fostered it and scattered it, and their successor, like the successors of Luther and Melanchthon, became so infected with the spirit of Rome that by 1844 the Protestant churches were morally like their mother.

In this we have been tracing the roots which bore the tree of education in the United States. While Harvard, the first school in New England, at first "was little more than a training school for ministers," and "the Bible was systematically studied," yet it is plain to any student of Harvard's course of study that, aside from Bible teaching, its curriculum was modeled after Eton, Rugby and other noted English schools which were all based on Sturm's system. Yale, William and Mary, and other institutions of the United States are modeled after this same system. *Behold Protestant America training her children in schools which were modeled after Sturm's Papal schools.*

The secret of the rejection of the Protestant denominations in 1844 is contained in the educational history just given. We see that, while they clung to the forms of Protestantism, their educational system continually instilled into the student the life of the Papacy. This produced a form of Protestantism imbued with the Papal spirit. This spells Babylon. *Should not our students seriously question the character of the educational system they are under,* lest they find themselves in the company of those five foolish virgins who are rejected in the time of the loud cry just as the great Christian churches were rejected at the time of the midnight cry because they failed to understand the "true science of education?" They did not "come into the line of true education," and they rejected the message.

Certain divine ideas of reform in civil government were received from God by some men in this country during the days of the wounding of the Papacy. These men dared teach and practice these truths. They fostered true principles of civil government to such an extent that the third angel's message could be delivered under its shelter. But the Papal system of education, as operated by Protestant churches, was a constant menace to this civil reform, because the churches would not break away from the mediaeval classical course with the granting of degrees and honors—without which it is difficult for aristocracy and imperialism in either church or state to thrive. But in spite of the failure of the churches to break away from this system, the civil reformers repudiated all crowns, titles, and honors that would have perpetuated European aristocracy and imperialism. The churches, because they still clung to the Papal educational system, became responsible, not only for the spirit of the Papacy within themselves, but also for the return of imperialism now so plainly manifesting itself in our government, and especially noticeable in such tendencies toward centralization as the trusts, monopolies and unions.

The year 1844 was one of the most critical periods in the history of the church since the days of the apostles. Toward that year the hand of prophecy had been pointing for ages. All heaven was interested in what was about to happen. Angels worked with intense interest for those who claimed to be followers of the Christ to prepare them to accept the message then due to the world. But the history quoted above shows that the Protestant denominations clung to the system of education borrowed from the Papacy which wholly unfitted them either to receive or give the message. Consequently, it was impossible for them to train men to proclaim it.

The world was approaching the great day of atonement in the heavenly sanctuary, the year 1844. Prior to this date, history records a most remarkable Christian educational movement and religious awakening. The popular churches were rapidly approaching their crucial test. And God knew it was impossible for them to acceptably carry the closing message unless they should "come into the line of true education"—unless they had a clear understanding of "the true science of education." These words were applicable to them, "Now as never before we need to understand the true science of education. If we fail to understand this, we shall never have a place in the kingdom of God." (Ellen G. White, *Christian Educator*, August 1, 1897).

What the Protestant churches faced in the year 1844, we Seventh-day Adventists are facing today. We shall see how the Protestant denominations opposed the principles of Christian education and thus failed to train their young people to give the midnight cry. Seventh-day Adventist young people, thousands of whom are in the schools of the world, cannot afford to repeat this failure. The moral fall of the popular churches causing that mighty cry, "Babylon is fallen, is fallen," would never have been given had they been true to the principles of Christian education. If individual Seventh-day Adventists approach the loud cry with the same experience that the Protestants approached the midnight cry, they likewise will be foolish virgins to whom the door is closed. The virgins in Christ's parable all had lamps, the doctrines; but they lacked a love of truth which lights up these doctrines. "The science of true education is the truth which is to be so deeply impressed on the soul that it cannot be obliterated by the error that everywhere abounds. The third angel's message is truth and light and power." (*Testimonies for the Church*, Vol. 6, p. 131). Is not Christian education, then, the light to the doctrines? Papal education fails to light up those lamps, for it is darkness.

Surely it is a serious time for our young Seventh-day Adventists—a time when every teacher in the land, when every student and prospective mission worker in the church, should look the situation squarely in the face and should determine his attitude toward the principles of Christian education. For "before we can carry the message of present truth in all its fulness to other countries, we must first break every yoke. We must come into the line of true education." (Ellen G. White, "The Madison School", *Special Testimonies*, Series B, No. 11, p. 30). "Now as never before we need to understand the true science of education. If we fail to understand this we shall never have a place in the kingdom of God." We are dealing with a life and death question.

2. History of Educational Reform Prior to 1844

❖

We now approach the study of the educational reform carried on among the Protestant denominations in connection with the first angel's message prior to 1844. The following statement shows that there was need of a reform in education at that time.

> "When the truth for these last days came to the world in the proclamation of the first, second and third angel's messages, we were shown that in the education of our children a different order of things must be brought in." (*Testimonies for the Church*, Vol. 6, p. 126).

It is impossible, in the limit of time, to study in detail all the experiences of the group of more than sixty schools advocating reform in education before 1844. With no attempt to exhaust the subject, the object will be to show that the light of Christian education shown with sufficient clearness in various schools of the United States to give the Protestant denominations an opportunity to gather up these principles as they were developing in the various schools, to incorporate them in their own church schools, to "come into the line of true education," and to train an army of missionaries to spread the message to the world at that time. For convenience, the various phases of Christian education will be considered as follows: The Place of the Bible in Education; Ancient and Modern Worldly Classics; Elective Courses of Study, Degrees, and Honors; Reforms in Diet, Location of Schools, and School Buildings; Training for Self-supporting Missionary Work and a Layman's Movement. The attitude of the Seventh-day Adventist student toward these problems will measure his efficiency in the proclamation of the third angel's message.

Historians quoted:—The history of the educational reform movement prior to 1844 from which we quote, has been written, in most part, by men not in sympathy with the reforms made at that time. Many of these schools, after relinquishing their reforms, developed the popular system of education. The educators connected with these schools in their later history are no more proud of that period which covers these reform experiences than is the man who has once known Christ, and has followed Him in simplicity, and has later gone to the world. Such a man is apt to make light of his religious experience, and excuse himself for his former attitude toward reform.

So these historians, writing after the reform period, have often pictured the reform in an unfavorable or even in a ridiculous light. Had we access to the reformers themselves, doubtless the movement would appear in a still stronger light. Enough is given, even by the enemies of the movement, to satisfy the reader that the Spirit of God did stir the hearts of educational and church leaders on these great reforms, and under its guidance they attempted to practice them.

THE PLACE OF THE BIBLE IN EDUCATION

Over this question, the relation the Word of God should sustain toward other subjects in the school curriculum, has been waged the war of educators for ages. The leader on each side in this controversy understands that his victory depends upon the position which the Bible holds in the school.

The story of this contest between the two forces over the position of God's Word in the education of the young may be read in the following Bible history:

> "The people served the Lord all the days of Joshua and all the days of the elders that outlived Joshua... And there arose another generation after them which knew not the Lord... and they forsook the Lord God ... and followed other gods, the gods of the people that were round about them, and bowed themselves unto them... And the anger of the Lord was hot against Israel, and he delivered them into the hands of spoilers that spoiled them ... so they could not any longer stand before their enemies ... Nevertheless the Lord raised up judges that delivered them... And it came to pass when the judge was dead they returned and corrupted themselves in following other gods." (Joshua 2:7-19).

This is a condensed history of ancient Israel. When the Word of God held its proper place in home and school, Israel was prosperous, and worldly nations said of them, "Surely this great nation is a wise and understanding people." Then we read that they would "forget the things" of God, and fail to "teach their children" the Word. These untaught children

> "mingled among the heathen, and learned their works, and they served their idols: which were a snare unto them... Thus were they defiled with their own works, and went a whoring with their own inventions... And he gave them into the hand of the heathen; and they that hated them ruled over them... Many times did he deliver them." (Psalm 106:35-43).

The student of the Bible can read in this history of ancient Israel a series of reforms which exalted the Word of God to its proper place in home and school. This was followed by carelessness in regard to Bible study and the practice of its principles in home and school. This meant that the ideas of worldly men took precedence of God's Word, resulting in such weakness that the very people whom Israel was so anxious to imitate despised them for their imitating, and regarded them with such disgust that they reduced Israel to abject slavery; and Israel lost the esteem of the world, in exchange for which she had neglected the Word of God. In the educational world she became the tail instead of the head. It has been a battle royal between Christ and Satan, Christ ever placing the wisdom of his Word before His people as "the principal thing," "a tree of life," while the god of this world holds us in bondage whenever the love of the truth dies out in our hearts. It has ever been his purpose to "spoil through philosophy and vain deceit after the tradition of men, after the rudiments of the world." And so the question at issue between Christ and Satan in the educational controversy, past, present, and future, has been concerning the place of the Bible in the minds and lives of teachers and students. The history of modern Israel may be written in the same language as ancient Israel, substituting only modern terms and phases to impress more vividly the comparisons and the applications. The generation beguiled into preferring worldly literature to the Word of God has seldom been able to apply these lessons to itself, because "the god of this world hath blinded the minds of them which believe not."

> "Above all other books, the Word of God must be our study, the great text book, the basis of all education; and our children are to be educated in the truths found therein, irrespective of previous habits and customs. In doing this, teachers and students will find the hidden treasure, the higher education. Bible rules are to be the guide of the daily life... A new purpose must be brought in and find place, and students must be aided in applying Bible principles in all they do. Whatever is crooked, whatever is twisted out of the right line is to be plainly pointed out and avoided, for it is iniquity not to be perpetuated." (*Testimonies for the Church*, Vol. 6, pp. 127, 131).

Students in our Christian schools should test every fact and statement offered by the Word of God. All information that does not stand the test should be rejected as chaff, for it is not oil for their lamps, and will only hinder in giving the loud cry. "A different order of things must be brought" into our schools, and "crooked and twisted things" must be straightened by Bible principles. Had this principle been followed prior to 1844 students would have been Prepared to receive the midnight cry, and to carry the message to the ends of the earth.

The Bible in Oberlin:—Oberlin College, established in Oberlin, Ohio, in the year 1833, had a most remarkable experience in the training of Christian workers. A historian of the institution writes,

> "The Scriptures both in the English version and in the original tongues were considered to possess the highest educational value, and as such, they should be studied first, last, and everywhere between... The Bible is fit to be and ought to be at least upon a par with the classics, and should have a place in every scheme of education from the primary school to the university... Should not the theological students read the entire Bible in Hebrew and Greek? Oberlin decided to restore the Bible to its place as a permanent text book in the whole course... Christian education without the Bible! A monstrosity in the religious world, a stumbling block to unbelievers!" (Delavan L. Leonard, *The Story of Oberlin*, p. 233-235 [The Pilgrim Press, 1898]).

The following words sum up the conclusions of a large class of scholarly men of that time who were endeavoring to bring about a reform in education:

> "In the dark ages the classics were first despised, then over-exalted, and the Scriptures belittled. Now, again, we see the Bible is good for style and taste... The Bible is overlooked and neglected in education.

Let the Bible have its place. *Matters like these are not to be decided by the customs of the schools which are yet replete with many a usage which has come from the age of Cardinal Bembo.*" (*Idem*, p. 235).

An earnest effort was made by many educational reformers to place the Bible where it belonged in the schools. The power of God attended this effort. Had not teachers yielded to the pressure brought by leaders who were in sympathy with worldly education, the history of the popular churches would have been entirely different, and that of Seventh-day Adventists also.

Oberlin allowed the Bible to slip from its exalted position, and, after a lapse of sixty years, from the following words we judge that the Bible has not yet reached the place it should occupy even with our own students:

"The Bible has not been made a standard matter in their education, but books mixed with infidelity, and propagating unsound theories, have been placed before them." (Ellen G. White, *Special Testimonies on Education*, p. 149).

ANCIENT AND MODERN WORLDLY CLASSICS

Students in a worldly system of education are inspired by ideas from the heathen classics and other worldly authors, even as students of Christian education are inspired by the Bible. The classics, or humanities, may not always appear by name in the curriculum of some so-called Christian schools, yet, if the system is not animated by the spirit of the Bible, the result of the education will be seen in worldly characters.

"Uninspired authors are placed in the hands of children and youth in our schools as lesson books—books from which they are to be educated. They are kept before the youth, taking up their precious time in studying those things which they can never use." (*Ibid.*, p. 232).

"All unnecessary matters need to be weeded from the course of study, and only such studies placed before the student as will be of real value to him." (*Ibid.*, p. 151).

The classics in Oberlin:—Educational reformers prior to 1844 endeavored to follow the truth in the subjects they taught. Oberlin among others had this experience:

"Heathen classics:—These two words stand for another of the burning questions of sixty years ago... The subject was under debate everywhere abroad." (*The Story of Oberlin*, p. 231).

President Mahan, in 1835,

"objected to the present plan in relation to Greek and Latin, especially the latter. It was better adapted, he said to educate the heathen than Christians. We can discipline the mind with the Hebrew and Greek Scriptures, and these can purify the mind. This is the opinion of the best men and the best scholars. Let us have less classics and more natural science, more American law, and history, more of men and things. Give us truth, facts, practical and available knowledge." (*Ibid.*, p. 232).

The annual announcement of Oberlin, issued in 1834, contains this statement,

"The collegiate department will afford as extensive instruction as other colleges, varying from some by substituting Hebrew and sacred classics for the most objectionable pagan authors."

The reason assigned for substituting the scripture in the original for heathen authors was "that certain classical authors were so abominably unclean that it is nothing less than criminal to put them into the hands of our youth." (*Idem*).

Sixty years after this, we Seventh-day Adventists received the following instruction on this subject, because our schools had not taken the positive stand on the classics and worldly authors that these educational reformers took prior to the midnight cry:

"Shall pagan and infidel sentiments be presented to our students as valuable additions to their store of knowledge?" (Ellen G. White, *Counsels to Parents, Teachers and Students*, p. 26).

The Board of Trustees asked the Faculty of Oberlin

"to consider with much prayer and deliberation whether the time devoted to heathen classics ought not to be improved by the study of the Hebrew Scriptures and natural science." (*The Story of Oberlin*, p. 233).

Three years later the same trustees asked,

"Should not the theological students read the entire Bible in Hebrew and Greek?" (*Idem*).

Two years later they voted,

> "that no student should be denied the approbation of the college at the end of his course by reason of any want of knowledge of heathen classics, provided he sustains well an examination in other branches needed to prepare him for preaching Christ." (*Idem*).

The movement to substitute the Scriptures for the heathen classics met with favor in many schools. In 1830 a lawyer of great eminence, a graduate of Yale, made a plea for "Sacred vs. Heathen Classics." The President of Amhurst, the President of Cooper Union, and Professor Stowe of Dartmouth College,

> "were in full sympathy with him in his desire to see relatively less honor bestowed upon the literature of ancient Greece and Rome, and relatively greater honor upon the literature of ancient Palestine." (*Ibid.*, p. 235).

These quotations show that a number of institutions of learning which today advocate the classics, at one time in their history favored the substitution of the Scriptures for the classics.

ELECTIVE COURSES OF STUDY AND DEGREES

Worldly education compels students, regardless of their needs or future work, to follow a prescribed course of instruction. It deals with students en masse. Christian education recognizes individual needs, and works to perfect individual character. It permits students, in counsel with teachers, to select subjects according to their future needs. The Papacy cannot thrive unless it puts students through a prescribed course, "the grind," to destroy independence and individuality. Protestantism is the reverse.

> "This long-drawn-out process, adding and adding more time, more branches, is one of Satan's snares to keep laborers back... If we had a thousand years before us, such a depth of knowledge would be uncalled for, although it might be much more appropriate; but now our time is limited." (*Special Testimonies on Education*, p. 106).

Elective courses:—Thomas Jefferson in his declaration of Principles for the University of Virginia in 1823, said, relative to the stereotype curriculum:

"I am not fully informed of the practices at Harvard, but there is one from which we shall certainly vary, although it has been copied, I believe, by nearly every college and academy in the United States. That is the holding the students all to one prescribed course of reading, and disallowing exclusive application to those branches only which are to qualify them for the particular vocations to which they are destined. We shall, on the contrary, allow them uncontrolled choice in the lectures they shall choose to attend, and require elementary qualifications only and sufficient age." (Herbert B. Adams, *Thomas Jefferson and the University of Virginia*, p. 123-124 [Government Printing Office, 1888]).

Boone further says,

"This policy has been in operation ever since... There is no curriculum of studies as in most institutions of like grade... This is 'the freedom of teaching;' ... and is the correlative of that ... equally fundamental 'freedom of learning' which in this country has come to be known as the 'open system,' or elective principle." (*Education in the United States*, pp. 190-191).

Jefferson's plan for an elective course was a blow at one of the fundamental principles of the Papal system which gives the student no choice, and, of course, was opposed by those controlled by the Papal system. Boone says, "In 1814, after numerous defeats and constant opposition from the already William and Mary College, from the Protestant churches, and from most of the political leaders of the time, Mr. Jefferson and his friends sought to provide... a university" which recognized the great principle of liberty in education. (*Idem*).

Randolph-Macon College, a Methodist institution, founded about 1828, grasped the light of Christian education and made an effort to break away from the mediaeval system which exalted the classics. Randolph-Macon took this action concerning the old mediaeval courses:

"The 'eclectic' system was adopted... It is claimed that more thorough work can be done under this system than under the old curriculum system. But students are not allowed to choose for themselves without consultation with the faculty. Practically, every student has a curriculum chosen for him according to the course he wishes to pursue." (*Thomas Jefferson and the University of Virginia*, p. 243).

Randolph-Macon had a hard time, and failed to carry out the reform. "It was a new movement, and it encountered prejudice or cold indifference on the part of the preachers and people." (*Ibid.*, p. 240).

Harvard, that school which imbibed the Papal system of John Sturm from the English Cambridge, and which led all other American schools in the Papal plan of education, was among the first of the older schools to attempt to come into line with true education on this reform. It began about 1824.

"'The experience of Harvard, during the long transition from a uniform required curriculum to a regulated freedom in choice of studies,' might be helpful to other institutions... There was adopted a course [described] as 'by far the broadest plan enacted up to that time.'" (*Education in the United States*, p. 192).

The students were given large latitude in their choice of studies. They were permitted to "elect from the following subjects... It was a large concession, and had a permanent influence upon the course." (*Idem*).

Yale, which so closely imitated Harvard in its early history, was materially effected by the reform in courses made by Harvard, and allowed students greater freedom in the choice of studies.

"Even Yale, which has been generally and very properly regarded as the conservator of the principle of authority in college instruction, has granted large liberty in a quarter of a century... So numerous were the concessions that 'nearly one-half of the work of the last two years,' ... 'was left to be determined by each student for himself.' ... [The] juniors [elected] about sixty per cent of their work, and seniors more than eighty per cent. From the standpoint of the ancient, or even of a scholar of the Revolutionary period, the change would seem to be ruinous. ... But no one longer denies either the necessity or the wisdom of the elective principle. 'To permit choice ... is dangerous; not to permit it is more dangerous.'" (*Ibid.*, pp. 197, 198).

The University of Michigan, years ago, loosened up, and "students were allowed to pursue special courses, and secure at their departure, certificates of proficiency."

Cornell University also grasped the principle of Christian education on the subject of elective courses. "Liberty in the choice of studies is regarded as fundamental." In many wide awake schools this question is being asked, "Shall a B.A. degree be given where the classics have been omitted? Johns Hopkins says, Yes." (*Ibid.*, pp. 197-198).

A prominent educator thus summarizes the virtues of the elective system: It encourages the early choice of one's life work; it develops individuality; it gives a chance for individual choice and guidance; it gives opportunity to teach what the student most needs; it best holds the interest of the student; it will early reveal the capacity of the student.

The old established courses were arbitrary, and were necessary to build up an educational trust suited to the needs of the Papacy. Without such courses it was difficult to adumbrate students, making them efficient tools in the hands of the leaders. No one should be allowed, according to their ideas of training, to exercise the right of choice, for fear he could not be directed as an obedient servant by the system when engaged in his life work. Individuality and personality, all independence and originality could be pretty well crushed by putting the students through the regular prescribed course of study. No man was allowed to teach, preach or do anything of importance without first finishing a course and receiving a degree.

So the Lord, in order to prepare workers for the midnight cry, inspired the reformers to attack the hard and fast course of study that had been inherited, practically without change from past centuries-a course that held the students' minds on the dim and musty past; that blinded them to the interesting and practical things of life and unfitted them to enter life capable of putting into practice the things learned in school. Such a training was absolutely useless to one preparing to give the midnight cry.

Degrees:—Christians must hold before the world "That all men are created equal; that they are endowed by their Creator with certain unalienable rights; that among these are life, liberty, and pursuit of happiness." The Papacy opposes these truths, and has found its most effective tools in overcoming these unalienable rights to be her educational system with its courses and degrees. On the one hand these destroy freedom, independence, and originality of thought, while on the other hand they develop class distinction, aristocracy and imperialism.

The apostate apostolic church in order to keep her members submissive to her will in teaching, found it necessary to develop an educational trust. This educational monopoly became effective and complete when she adopted the pagan scheme of rigid courses leading to degrees. She gave the form to Christianity, and for the Spirit of God she substituted the pagan spirit. The combination of Christian form and pagan life produced the Papacy. Hartman, writing concerning the educational system of the apostate church, says, "The conferring of degrees was originated by a pope." (Rev. B. Hartman, *Religion or No Religion in Education*, p. 43).

> "Many who professed conversion still clung to the tenets of their pagan philosophy, and not only continued its study themselves, but urged it upon others as a means of extending their influence among the heathen." (*Great Controversy*. p. 508).

> "As long as we sail with the current of the world, we need neither canvas nor oar. It is when we turn squarely about to stern the current that our labors begin, and Satan will bring every kind of theory to pervert the truth. The work will go hard." (*Testimonies for the Church*, Vol. 6, p. 129).

> "There is need of heart conversion among the teachers. A genuine change of thought and methods of teaching is required to place them where they will have a personal relation to a living Saviour." (Ellen G. White, *Fundamentals of Christian Education*, p. 435).

Thomas Jefferson, the man who wrote that grand old document, The Declaration of Independence, which announced to the world our separation from the Papal form of government, and which enunciates the divine principle that all men are created free and equal, endeavored to develop an educational system in harmony with the reform position which the government had assumed. He saw the necessity of discarding rigid courses and degrees, and introduced the "elective system" as we have seen.

> "At first he attempted to drop the long established academic titles, save that of M.D. and to adopt the simple title of Graduate U.V., the name of the school or schools in which the student 'had been declared eminent,' being expressed in his 'certificate,' which was to be 'attested' by the particular professor." (*Thomas Jefferson and the University of Virginia*, p. 153).

Professor Tappan, first president of the University of Michigan, followed Jefferson's plan. "Students were allowed to pursue special courses, and receive at their departure certificates of proficiency." (*Education in the United States*, p. 191).

That "first attempts to change old customs brought severe trials," (Ellen G. White, *Testimonies for the Church*, Vol. 6, p. 141) was well illustrated in the experience of the founders in the University of Virginia, for "in a few years the Board and Faculty were forced to give up the reform."

We have seen that the popular demand for the old established course and degrees was too strong for Jefferson to withstand. Later the spirit of God stirred the churches by setting up an agitation in the Oberlin school, giving them an opportunity to get away from that system so effective in maintaining the Papacy, and to prepare the people of God for the midnight cry. Of Oberlin College it is said,

> "The democratic feeling, the spirit of equality, the absence of classes and castes, based upon mere artificial distinctness is almost as marked in the institution as in the village." (*The Story of Oberlin*, p. 398).

> "There has been no positive action by trustees or faculty in opposition to such degrees, only traditional repugnance. Even the common degrees, in course, have been sometimes held in disrepute among the students. Half of the class of 1838, which numbered twenty, declined to receive the degree and the President announced at the commencement that those who desired the degree could receive their diplomas at the college office." (James H. Fairchild, *Oberlin: The Colony and the College*, p. 267).

The pressure of the church controlling Oberlin was so strong that the reformers were unable to break away from the old educational system. Who can tell how much weight this failure had in reducing the Protestant churches to the condition called "Babylon?"

EMULATION, HONORS AND PRIZES

The granting of degrees, prizes, honors, etc., is borrowed from the Papal system of education.

> "In our institutions of learning there was to be exerted an influence that would counteract the influence of the world, and give no encouragement to indulgence in appetite, in selfish gratification of the senses, in pride, ambition, love of dress and display, love of praise and flattery, and strife for high rewards and honors as a recompense for good scholarship. All this was to be discouraged in our schools. It

would be impossible to avoid these things and yet send them to the public school." (Ellen G. White, *Review and Herald*, Jan. 9, 1894).

Before 1844 God was endeavoring to do for the Protestant denominations what he is now endeavoring to do for Seventh-day Adventists. The educational reform prior to the midnight cry proved a failure. But he who shares in the loud cry must succeed in the educational reform.

> "Oberlin is somewhat peculiar in the matter of marks, prizes, honors and the like. During the thirties when Mr. Shipherd and his associates were laying the foundations, there was much earnest discussion abroad concerning the value and legitimacy of emulation... in student life. Many of the foremost educators held most strenuously that they are not needed to secure the best results, while in general tendencies it was on the whole positively harmful and vicious. In every way it was far better to appeal to pupils of all grades as well as to all others by addressing only their higher nature. Influenced largely by such convictions, it has always been that, though recitations and examinations are marked and a record is kept, this is not to establish a basis for grading or for distribution of honors, but only for private consultation by the teacher, a student, or other persons concerned. No announcement of standing is ever made." (*The Story of Oberlin*, p. 408).

University of Nashville:—While Oberlin was struggling over the question of prizes, rewards, classics, etc., other institutions were battling with the same problem. Doctor Lindsley, founder of the University of Nashville, the predecessor of the well-known Peabody Institute, established in this period, said, "The giving of prizes as rewards for scholarship was discarded," and the founder testifies. that "a much greater peace, harmony, contentment, order, industry, and moral decorum prevailed." (Lucius S. Marriam, *Higher Education in Tennessee*, p. 33).

Horace Mann, the eminent teacher and writer, and the father of the public school system in the United States, heartily disapproved of the classic system of emulation. Mr. Mann says,

> "I hold and always have held it too unchristian to place two children in such relation to each other that if one wins the other must lose. So placed, what scholars gain in intellect, yes, and a thousand times more, they lose in virtue... You know my view of emulation. It may make bright scholars, but it makes rascally politicians and knavish merchants." (Marie Tyler e Horace Mann, *Life and Works of Horace Mann*, vol. 1, pp. 494, 515).

Mr. Mann was opposing the Jesuit Papal practice, so necessary to the success of their system of education, which, says,

> "Nothing will be held more honorable than to outstrip a fellow student and nothing more dishonorable than to be outstripped. Prizes will be distributed to the best pupils with the greatest possible solemnity." (*A History of Education*, p. 171).

REFORMS IN DIET

"The true science of education" gives the student a knowledge of the laws governing his body, and a love for those laws. Every Christian school should give its students a knowledge of the proper diet, proper clothing, and should acquaint him with those phases of life that make a successful missionary. A wave of reform in the matters of diet, clothing, and other important health principles swept over the country, and many educational reformers endeavored to introduce these practical subjects into their schools. The spirit of God was preparing them for the crucial test in 1844.

> "Among the studies selected for childhood, physiology should occupy the first place." (Ellen G. White, *The Health Reformer*, August 1, 1866, par. 4).
>
> "It should be regarded as the basis of all educational effort." (*Ibid.*, November 1, 1871, par. 3).
>
> "While the schools we have established have taken up the study of physiology, they have not taken hold with the decided energy they should. They have not practiced intelligently that which they have received in knowledge." (Ellen G. White, *Healthful Living*, p. 13 [1897]).
>
> "The health should be as sacredly guarded as the character." (Ellen G. White, *Christian Education*, p. 184).

The founders of Oberlin, moved by the spirit of reform said,

> "That we may have time and health for the Lord's service, we will eat only plain and wholesome food, renouncing all bad habits, and especially the smoking and chewing of tobacco, unless it is necessary as a medicine, and deny ourselves all the strong and unnecessary drinks, even tea and coffee, as far as practicable, and everything expensive that is simply calculated to gratify appetite." (*The Story of Oberlin*, p. 86).

In 1832, Mr. Sylvester Graham, the inventor of graham flour,

> "began to call men to repent of the sins of the table. According to this classical authority, vegetables and fruit should constitute the substance of every meal, and should be eaten as nearly as may be in their natural state. Bread should be made of unbolted wheat flour (that being the natural condition), though rye and Indian are allowable if unbolted, likewise rice and sago, if plainly cooked. Good cream may be used instead of butter, though milk and honey are somewhat better. Flesh meat and fish in all forms had better be banished from the table. No fat or gravies are to be tasted, nor any liquid foods like soup and broth. Pastry is an abomination, and cakes in which any fat or butter has been used. Bread should be at least twelve hours from the oven, and twenty-four hours are better. And as for condiments, pepper, mustard, oil, vinegar, etc., and stimulants like tea and coffee, they are to be by all means eschewed as deadly foes to health." (*Ibid.*, pp. 218-219).

Professors Shipherd and Finney of Oberlin both confessed to being restored to health through the Graham diet reform. "The Oberlin pulpit became aggressively Grahamite. The boarding department of the school was placed in charge of a disciple of Graham. "Tea and coffee were not introduced into the college boarding hall until 1842-possibly a little later... Many of the families discarded tea and coffee, and a few adopted the vegetarian diet." Concerning the vegetarian diet, we read,

> "For two or three years longer the students were furnished at the hall with 'Graham fare.' They were not restricted to this. A table was still set for those who preferred a different diet." (*Oberlin: The Colony and the College*, p. 83).

Diet reform in other schools:—Oberlin was not along in these reforms. "In Williams College an association was formed in 1831 comprising the majority of the students with board based upon the principles of abstinence from tea and coffee, and the use only of food, the simplest in every respect." "The same reform was recorded in the history of Hudson College." In Lane Seminary "it was the wish of the students to dispense with tea, coffee, and all luxuries, and to live on the principles of Christian simplicity and economy." "In Danville, Ky., and Maryville College, Tennessee, it was the same, because we wish our ministers free from dyspepsia and liver complaint." Oberlin's historian writes that "the company was large that used neither flesh nor fish, neither butter nor milk, neither tea nor coffee." (*The Story of Oberlin*, 222, 223).

Horace Mann said,

> "We must pay far more attention to the health of the students, not only by teaching the physiological laws of health, but by training students to an habitual obedience to them. Solomon does not say *teach* a child the way he should go, but he says "*train*" him, which means that the child shall be required to do the thing himself, and to repeat it again and again, and ten times again, until it becomes a habit." (George C. Mann, *Life and Works of Horace Mann*, Vol. 5, [1891], p. 415).

Mr. Mann says further,

> "As physical exercise enters so largely into the means of securing health, it is certain that no college can ever maintain a general condition of high health among its students unless they spend some hours every day in muscular effort. Hence the Faculty of Antioch College requires exercise of its students every day... We encourage manual labor in every practicable way, and if a liberal public or a liberal individual would give us land for agricultural or even for horticultural purposes, we promise them that the old injunction to till the ground and dress it shall not be forgotten." (*Ibid.*, pp. 415, 416).

One will look far for a writer with a clearer grasp of the health principles as taught by the Word of God. After describing the increase of disease in the world because of the departure of man from God's original plan, Mr. Mann says,

> "[It comes] solely because man will break heaven's laws; because, for the sake of money, or for pride, disease will marry disease; ... because when God commanded Adam *to work*—that is, to take some form of exercise—*in the garden*—that is, in the open air—men will not exercise, and will live in dwellings which add artificial poisons to natural ones, and then breathe the virulent compound." (*Ibid.*, p. 341).

If health reform must be taught by Seventh-day Adventist ministers and teachers, and understood and practiced by all who will triumph in the loud cry, we are forced to conclude that the Lord was giving the Protestant churches, through their schools, this health reform light because it was as necessary for them to understand and practice it before the midnight cry as for us before the loud cry. We are forced also to conclude that their failure to live up to the light on health reform unfitted them to appreciate and accept other light. So it is extremely dangerous for students now to carelessly relate themselves to this reform.

THE PROPER LOCATION FOR SCHOOLS AND COUNTRY LIFE FOR STUDENTS

The Papal system of education is typified by the word centralization; it exalts man, his ideas and his ways. In other words it is a study of the humanities, of the artificial rather than the natural. Such a scheme of education can best be worked out in connection with city life. Therefore, Papal schools and those schools patterned after the Papal model are usually located in towns and cities. On the contrary, Christian education means decentralization; it exalts God and His works; it is a return to God's way of doing. This system can best be developed in the country, on a farm where is to be gained an experience necessary to the carrying of the last message.

> "God bids us establish schools away from the cities, where, without let or hindrance, we can carry on the work of education upon plans that are in harmony with the solemn message that is committed to us for the world. Such an education as this can best be worked out where there is land to cultivate... The usefulness learned on the school farm is the very education that is most essential for those who go out as missionaries to many foreign fields." ("The Madison School," pp. 28-29).

> "Some do not appreciate the value of agricultural work. These should not plan for our schools, for they will hold everything from advancing in right lines. In the past their influence has been a hindrance." (*Testimonies for the Church*, Vol. 6, p. 178).

Concerning the school grounds it is said,

> "This land is not to be occupied with buildings, except to provide the facilities essential for the teachers and students of the school. This land about the school is to be reserved as the school farm. It is to become a living parable to the students. The students are not to regard the school land as a common thing... They are to plant it with ornamental and fruit trees and to cultivate garden produce... The school farm is to be regarded as a lesson book in nature... (*Ibid.*, pp. 181, 182).

Bring all your energies into the development of the Lord's farm... (*Ibid.*, pp. 192).

The reasons that have led us in a few places to turn away from cities and locate our schools in the country, hold good with the schools in other places... Had the money which our larger schools have used in expensive buildings been invested in procuring land where students could receive a proper education, so large a number of students would not now be struggling under the weight of increasing debt, and the work of these institutions would be in a more prosperous condition... The students would have secured an all-round education which would have prepared them, not only for practical work in various trades, but for a place on the Lord's farm in the earth made new." (*Ibid.*, p. 177).

We have seen that God was endeavoring to arouse the popular churches to accept Christian education. This meant a reform in the location of their schools. A few years prior to 1844, many educational reformers were influenced to establish schools away from the city and on the farm.

The Methodists as early as 1735 under the direction of the Wesleys and Whitefield attempted to carry out God's idea of education in Georgia. They established a school ten miles from Savannah. The historian states, "Mr. Habbersham had located the five hundred acre grant." Wesley stated that this school should be "a seat and nursery of sound learning and religious education."

The University of Virginia on a farm:—When Thomas Jefferson was making plans for the University of Virginia in a report made

"to the Speaker of the House of Delegates, it is stated that they purchased 'at a distance of a mile from Charlottesville... two hundred acres of land, on which was an eligible site for the college, high, dry, open, furnished with good water, and nothing in its vicinity which could threaten the health of the students.'" (*Thomas Jefferson and the University of Virginia*, p. 69).

Oberlin on a farm:—Mr. Shipherd, the founder of Oberlin College, writes thus of his early plans,

"We are to establish schools of the first order, from the infant school up to an academic school, which shall afford a thorough education in English and useful languages, and if Providence favor it, at length instruction in theology—I mean practical theology. We are to connect work shops and the farm with the institution." (*Oberlin: the colony and the college*, p. 18).

A tract of land was purchased in the unbroken forests of Ohio, and 640 acres of this were kept for school purposes. The soil was clay and wet, and the tract "had been passed by for years as undesirable for occupation." For this very reason the purchase was severely criticized. It was made because the faith of the founders enabled them to see some things that even land experts overlooked. Let Seventh-day Adventists read the similar experience of the founders of the Avondale school, Cooranbong, Australia. The founders of Oberlin

> "were guided by a wisdom higher than human, since a location, almost forbidding in its physical aspects, and for years quite difficult of access, was a condition indispensable to the formation of the character and the performance of the work to which Oberlin was clearly called." (*The Story of Oberlin*, p. 82).

Richmond College (Virginia) was founded by the Baptists in 1832.

> "[They] bought Spring Farm, a small tract some four miles northwest of the city, and there on the Fourth of July, opened a manual labor school, called the Virginia Baptist Seminary." (*Thomas Jefferson and the University of Virginia*, p. 271).

Emory and Henry College, a Methodist institution, was established in Virginia in 1835. It was to be

> "what was called, a manual labor college, an institution of learning in which the pupils were to be trained to labor as well as to think. This manual labor feature was a very prominent one in the enterprise, as it was first brought before the public... A farm containing six hundred acres of highly productive land was purchased and paid for out of the first funds raised. It was at first intended that this farm should be cultivated by student labor, for which a compensation was to be allowed which would assist in paying the student's expenses." (*Ibid.*, pp. 253-254).

It would be interesting to study this reform further for many other schools followed this light and secured locations away from towns and cities. When manual training is studied this phase of educational reform will be brought again to your attention.

SIMPLICITY IN BUILDINGS

Reform in education includes the buildings in which an educational institution is housed. The spirit of centralization is a necessary feature of the Papacy, and associated with the Papal educational system of mediaeval Europe there is usually found a certain characteristic form of buildings—buildings of the monastic order, dark, dingy cloisters, with which are associated long prayers, counting of beads, chained Bibles, cowls, gowns, mortar boards, night vigils, long examinations, degrees, parchment rolls; memory work instead of reason; sight not faith; thought not action. Rosenkranz says,

> "Monkish education seeks by means of complete silence to place the soul in a state of immobility, which, through the want of all interchange of thought, at last sinks into entire apathy and antipathy toward all intellectual culture." (*The Philosophy of Education*, p. 256).

Think of attempting to give this kind of education in the open, free country, or in buildings with open windows through which streams the bright sunshine of heaven, surrounded by singing birds, working teams, milk cows, growing grain, and the sound of hammer and saw. Such surroundings kill this system of education as surely as light kills germs.

> "The mistakes that have been made in the erection of buildings in the past should be salutary admonitions to us in the future... Our ideas of building and furnishing our institutions are to be molded and fashioned by a true, practical knowledge of what it means to walk humbly with God. Never should it be thought necessary to give an appearance of wealth. ... It is not large, expensive buildings; it is not rich furniture ... that will give our work influence and success." (*Testimonies for the Church*, Vol. 7, pp. 92, 93).

Thomas Jefferson in his scheme for giving a democratic education discarded the mediaeval dormitory system of Papal schools.

> "Instead of constructing a single and large edifice which might have exhausted their funds, and left nothing or too little for other essential expenses, they thought it better to erect a small and separate building for each professor with an apartment for his lectures, and others for their own accommodations, connecting these cottages, by a range of dormitories capable each of lodging two students only—a provision

equally friendly to study as to morals and order." (*Thomas Jefferson and the University of Virginia*, p. 69).

Of the students' cottages it is said, "They consisted of one story dormitories exhibiting a not unpleasant effect," and these buildings had their "garden grounds."

This certainly called for self-government. It placed teachers and students on the same level; it encouraged simplicity of life; it was economical, and appeals strongly to those who are limited in the amount of money they can spend in school buildings and equipments. But still other reasons are given for this cottage plan. Jefferson said,

> "The plan offered the further advantages of greater security against fire and infection, of extending the buildings in equal pace with the funds, and of adding to them indefinitely hereafter... Instead of one immense building, [I favor] to have a small one for every professorship, arranged at proper distances around a square, to admit of extension, connected by a piazza, so that they may go dry from one school to another. This village form is preferable to a single great building for many reasons, particularly on account of fire, health, economy, peace, and quiet. ... Such a plan had been approved in the case of the Albemarle College." (*Ibid.*, pp. 69, 73).

> "Cabell also was thoroughly convinced of the soundness of the building policy of the University. Even the enemies of the institution acknowledged that Jefferson's course was wise. ... [An influential visitor] had been won over to the university by a mere visit of inspection which impressed him with the extent and splendor of the establishment... There was absolutely nothing in the neighborhood of Charlottesville to attract either professors or students. Jefferson was compelled, by the necessities of the situation, to create something visible and impressive which should compel admiration." (*Ibid.*, p. 100).

Before the opening of the university, Jefferson wrote of ten distinct houses for the professors, "each with a garden," and "an hundred-and-nine dormitories sufficient each for two students." (*Ibid.*, p. 101).

Jefferson saw the effect of architecture on the plastic minds of students, and said,

> "My partiality for that division is not founded in views of education solely, but infinitely more as the means of a better administration of our government, and the eternal preservation of republican principles." (*Ibid.*, p. 73).

Oberlin's founders came into line with the truth in the matter of simple buildings.

> "To increase our means of service ... we will observe plainness and durability in the construction of our houses, furniture, carriages, and all that appertains to us." (*The Story of Oberlin*, p. 86).

> "There is a plain, neat, simple style of building which commends itself to every man's enlightened good sense, and still will not be highly esteemed by the world, neither is it an abomination in the sight of the Lord." (*Oberlin: The Colony and the College*, p. 359).

The cottage plan for housing students was followed by other schools also. Of Oglethorpe University, one of the leading Presbyterian institutions in the early history of Georgia, it is said,

> "There was a row of dormitories of one-story for the habitation of students... These were placed twelve feet apart and each one was divided into two rooms eighteen feet square." (Charles E. Jones, *Education in Georgia*, p. 83).

This was in 1837 when Presbyterians were wrestling with the "true science of education," and were settling the question whether they would help proclaim the last message to the world. The object of the Christian school is to train young people to "endure hardness as good soldiers of Jesus Christ." Worldly governments, when training soldiers, avoided those conveniences and luxuries that tend to make the soldiers unwilling to endure the hardships of the battlefield. They are not quartered in up-to-date hotels. But often the buildings of a school are constructed and equipped for the convenience of those who teach, house and board the students, rather than for the training necessary to fit these young people to become soldiers to endure hardness. The uniform, the manners, and the polishing in general, of the young student soldier receive more attention than actual drill from many of the officers who have had more experience in dress parade than in lying in the trenches. Need we wonder why such a large per cent of the students, after long training, prefer to take up work in an institution with up-to-date conveniences where good food, clothes, and a salary are insured, rather than to pioneer an enterprise where they are thrown largely on their own resources? To what extent are large, well-equipped schools responsible for this? In these last days schools that teach students to be content with simple food and clothing, and encourage the spirit of sacrifice, and give the ability to say, "From henceforth that land is my country which most needs my help," will be in greatest demand by those students who expect to triumph in the loud cry.

It was on this principle that Thomas Jefferson constructed simple school buildings in which to train a class of men to promote the principles of democracy in the United States. And practically every government in the world has been effected by these principles.

The average teacher, when thinking of a training school, conceives of large buildings, equipped with modern facilities and conveniences, calling for a large outlay of means. You students have had no such plant before you here. Your school would scarcely be recognized as an educational institution by one having the ordinary conception of a training school. This chapel, the small recitation rooms, the dining room, the shops, cottages, and other buildings grouped about the farm, provide the school facilities. Our facilities are, as a rule, more simple than many of you have in your own homes. What is the result? Scores of students from this plant have caught a vision, and have recognized the possibility of building up a school with limited means. As a result, over thirty little centers are providing education to hundreds of children outside the church, while if these same students had received their training in a school well equipped and expensive, no doubt the number of schools started would be considerably less.

Again, the average person when thinking of a sanitarium has before his mind one of our large institutions with every modern convenience. You have had before you a small sanitarium consisting of three frame, one-story cottages connected by covered porches, equipped so simply that they can be duplicated in almost any mission. You have seen this sanitarium filled with patients and a list of persons waiting admittance. Many have had their ideas revolutionized by this small sanitarium, and several health homes are coming into existence to be conducted on similar plans.

These two illustrations are cited to show that the effects of surrounding buildings and equipments on the minds of students are beyond calculation. The light was given to the Protestants before 1844 to guide them in the erection of buildings, equipment and furnishings; in diet, dress and surroundings, so that a great army might be able, in a simple manner to sweep the earth with that mighty message, the midnight cry.

MANUAL TRAINING AND THE PRACTICAL IN EDUCATION

The times demand an education which will produce men and women capable of doing things. The Papal system divorces learning from doing and disqualifies men and women for giving the final warning to the world. God stirred every denomination, prior to 1844, to put practical Christian education within the reach of the young people.

> "Had the system of education generations back been conducted upon altogether a different plan, the youth of this generation would not now be so depraved and worthless... There should have been in past generations provisions made for education upon a larger scale. In connection with the schools should have been agricultural and manufacturing establishments. There should have been teachers also of household labor... If schools had been established upon the plan we have mentioned, there would not now be so many unbalanced minds. I have been led to inquire, Must all that is valuable in our youth be sacrificed in order that they may obtain an education at the schools? If there had been agricultural and manufacturing establishments in connection with our schools, and competent teachers had been employed to educate the youth in the different branches of study and labor, devoting a portion of each day to mental improvement, and a portion of the day to physical labor, there would now be a more elevated class of youth to come upon the stage of action, to have influence in molding society. The youth who would graduate at such institutions would many of them come forth with stability of character. They would have perseverance, fortitude, and courage to surmount obstacles, and principles that would not be swerved by wrong influence, however popular. There should have been experienced teachers to give lessons to young ladies in the cooking department. Young girls should have been instructed to manufacture wearing apparel, to cut, to make, to mend garments, and thus become educated for the practical duties of life." (*Christian Education*, pp. 11, 18, 19).

Jefferson, as we might expect, caught a glimpse of this important phase of education, and made an attempt to put it into operation in the University of Virginia.

> "He proposed what he called a 'School of Technical Philosophy'... To such a school will come the mariner, carpenter, shipwright, pump-maker, clockmaker, mechanist, optician, founder, cutler, ... soapmaker, tanner, saltmaker, glassmaker, to learn as much as shall be necessary to pursue their art understandingly... In this school of technology, Jefferson proposed to group the students in convenient classes for elementary and practical instruction by lectures, to be given in the evening, so as to afford an opportunity for labor in the daytime." (*Thomas Jefferson and the University of Virginia*, p. 84).

Jefferson is quoted as saying, "No nation will long survive the decay of its agriculture." (Samuel H. Comings, *Pagan vs. Christian Civilizations*, p. 43).

The "Society for Promoting Manual Labor in Literary Institutions" was formed in New York in 1831 "with nearly a score of eminent names among its officers."

> "A tremendous impulse was given to the movement by the publication, in 1833, of Theodore D. Welds' famous pamphlet upon manual labor, under the auspices of the [society]... It contained the testimony of hundreds of noted men, all to the effect that this panacea without question was mighty to heal... His report... when published produced one of the sensations of the time." (*The Story of Oberlin*, pp. 230, 130).

Manual labor in Oberlin:—Oberlin was among the schools of this period that placed themselves in the hands of God to be used in giving a practical education to hundreds and thousands of youth who would later be called to do strenuous service for the Master. The historian of Oberlin states that about the time that school started, there was "a widespread intellectual quickening, including radical reforms in educational methods." Mr. Shipherd, one of the founders of Oberlin, desired to be in harmony with the divine plan of education, and said,

> "Hundreds of promising youth will doubtless be educated for God's service, or not educated, as we shall or shall not provide for them the means of complete education by their own industry and economy." (*Oberlin: The Colony and the College*, p. 321).

In the first annual report of Oberlin published in 1834, we read, "The manual labor department is considered indispensable to a complete education." (*The Story of Oberlin*, p. 224). The historian states,

> "Honest toil would be honored, the richest and poorest would meet daily on a common level, the health of all would be secured, a magic stimulus would be imparted to both minds and morals; but the best of all, and most certain of all, whoever of either sex would gain an education could easily pay his way with the labor of his own hands." (*Idem*).

Oberlin's industrial department, the historian says,

> "is furnished with a steam engine which propels a saw mill, grist mill, shingle and lath saw, and turning lathe, to which other machinery will be added. One workshop is now erected and supplied with tools, and others are to be added." (*Idem*).

> "Manual labor was among the most indispensable elements of the Oberlin idea. Nothing did more for Oberlin's establishment and enlargement. For half a generation multitudes of students were brought in from the whole land over, who otherwise would never have entered its halls; and much more, in all probability, would never have gained an education." (*Ibid.*, pp. 100, 101).

One of Oberlin's founders in 1833 wrote

> "that a female department would be established on the manual labor plan, including housekeeping, manufacture of wool, culture of silk, appropriate parts of gardening, particularly the raising of seeds for market, making clothes, etc." (*Ibid.*, pp. 225, 226).

In fact, the object of Oberlin, as published in its first circular and first catalog [1834], is said to be:

> "'to give the most *useful* education at the least expense of health, time and money; to extend the benefit of such education to both sexes and to all classes of the community. ... The thorough qualification of Christian teachers both for the pulpit and for schools;' ... 'the diffusion of useful science, sound morality, and pure religion among the growing multitudes of the Mississippi Valley, and to the destitute millions which overspread the world,' through ministers and 'pious school-teachers.'" (*Ibid.*, p. 161).

Manual labor met with intense opposition, but in 1833, Mr. Shipherd wrote jubilantly,

"The scholars study and work well. Five minutes after the manual labor bell strikes, the hammers and saws of the mechanical students wake all around us." (*Ibid.*, p. 224).

After naming the advantages of manual training, he adds,

"In a word, it meets the wants of man as a compound being, and prevents the common and amazing waste of money, time, health and life." (*Idem*).

Numerous manual labor institutions:—

"In all this Oberlin was not in the least original, but merely copied, with slight modifications, what was to be found in numerous institutions throughout the eastern, middle and western states. In 1830, ten could be named having manual labor attachments, while during the next decade several scores were added to the number. Maine Wesleyan was famous in its day and was among the earliest, while Bowdoin, Waterville, and Bangor Seminary possessed these advantages. In Dexter, Maine, not only all students, but teachers also were required to labor at least four hours each day. Massachusetts had at least half a dozen... New York was favored with several, Oneida Institute being prominent; and the Rochester Institute of Practical Education, in which students of ordinary mechanical skill while learning a trade can nearly pay their board, and it is calculated, when certain intended facilities are furnished, they will pay all their expenses. Pennsylvania, too, was well supplied. At Lafayette College, Easton, President Jenkins and the students performed the labor of erecting a two-story building... In the west where people were poorer and land was cheaper, manual labor was most popular. Hudson (Ohio) had shops and a farm, Marietta and Lane Seminary the same, with at least as many more. Michigan moved in the great matter while yet a territory, nor were Indiana, Illinois, Kentucky, or Tennessee, in the least degree backward in ministering to the muscle of the student class." (*Ibid.*, pp. 229-230).

"The educational societies of all the leading denominations were active participants, whether Baptist, Congregational, Episcopal, Methodist, or Presbyterian, and most of the leading educators were full of enthusiasm and zeal... The Episcopalian secretary could exclaim: 'We almost envy our successors in the academic course when something of the vigor of the fathers shall be found in the intellectual laborers of the day, and the sallow tinge of dyspepsia shall cease to be the uniform testimonial of a life of study.'" (*Ibid.*, p. 230).

Dr. Lindsley, founder of the University of Nashville, now Peabody Institute, was an advocate of manual labor.

> "[He] would have attached to schools of all grades, farms and workshops. These farms and workshops would serve a three-fold purpose. They would furnish the needed exercise, they would be useful in teaching trades, and they would give poor boys an opportunity of making a living." (*Higher Education in Tennessee*, p. 30).

Emory and Henry College, in 1835, was

> "a manual labor college, an institute of learning in which the pupils were to be trained to labor as well as think. This manual labor feature was a very prominent one in the enterprise... This feature was made prominent in these incipient movements, for the institution was built up by a people engaged almost wholly in agriculture and the mechanic arts, a people among many of whom a prejudice existed against a learned and lazy race." (*Thomas Jefferson and the University of Virginia*, p. 253).

Manual training in Baptist schools:—

> "In 1830, a few devoted men met in the Second Baptist Church at five o'clock a. m. to devise and propose some plan for the improvement of young men who, in the judgment of the churches, were called to the work of the ministry... They organized the Virginia Baptist Educational Society, and for two years aided approved young men by placing them in private schools ... In 1832, the Society bought Spring Farm... opened a manual labor school, called the Virginia Baptist Seminary... The number of students ran up to twenty-six, about thirds of them preparing for the ministry... To this purchase of nine acres, six more were added in 1836... The design in adding more was to give more scope for the manual labor feature of the school. This was strenuously insisted on by the authorities as giving to the needy opportunity for self-help and to all opportunity for exercise. But it proved unpopular with the students... And finally as we read in the report of 1841, this feature ... has been virtually abandoned." (*Ibid.*, p. 271).

The Georgia Baptists in 1833 founded Mercer University, a school

> "which would unite agricultural labor with study, and be open for those only preparing for the ministry. The idea of founding a manual labor school where theory and practice should be taught, a scheme much in favor with Georgia Baptists, seems to have originated with Doctor Sherwood, who was the first to demonstrate its feasibility in the academy established by him near Eatonton in Putnam County." (*Education in Georgia*, p. 61).

We might multiply historical data concerning manual training schools during this remarkable educational reform preceding 1844. The examples given are typical of the experiences of more than sixty manual training schools of this period. To Seventh-day Adventist educational reformers, these experiences are thrilling. What would have been the results had the men responsible for these earlier reforms the pressure brought to bear upon them by the leading brethren of their respective denominations? This opposition was hard to meet, but the failure of the cause was really due to lack of courage and devotion to these principles, for where there is intense courage and love for God's work, opposition only strengthens the reformers. Adventists know that angels were busy everywhere encouraging these reforms. It is a startling fact that these schools relinquished their hold on the manual training reform just about the time that the midnight cry was due. Had they remained true, history would have made a different story. The history of Seventh-day Adventist educational work also would have been different.

Had Oberlin, for instance, remained true to her manual training idea, her missionary workers, going as they did to the mountaineers of the South and to the freedmen of the South, would have changed the whole complexion of Southern history. It would have placed the Southern states forty years ahead of the present. Booker T. Washington's work for negroes would have been established a quarter of a century before his time. But

> "because men could not comprehend the purpose of God in the plans laid before us for the education of workers, methods have been followed in some of our schools which have retarded rather than advanced the work of God. Years have passed into eternity with small results that might have shown the accomplishment of a great work." ("The Madison School," p. 29).

Advantages of manual labor:—

> "The students were divided into small companies of eight or ten each, and each company placed under the supervision of one of the older students... It broke the monotony of ordinary student life; it promoted health and buoyancy of spirit; in the hours of field and forest labor, there was found not only relief from study but such a variety of incident, that the students of those days found more means of solid enjoyment than others have since... All the students except

day students boarded in a common hall, where by practicing economy and with the help of the farm, a variable surplus was realized each year which was applied in making improvements." (*Thomas Jefferson and the University of Virginia*, p. 253-255).

Manual labor, as a part of the curriculum in those schools training ministers and missionary workers, is a part of that "science of true education" which God made known to some men and women prior to the year 1844. It was one of God's ways of training practical missionaries for mission fields of the world. In spite of the fact that practically every Protestant denomination had some experience in conducting manual training schools, these denominations as a whole opposed the idea, and their persistent opposition finally forced the schools that had led out in the reform to close their manual labor departments. The closing of the manual labor departments is a signal for a return to the educational system of mediaeval Europe. They began to train worldlings instead of Christians. Herein lay one of the greatest mistakes of the Protestant denominations prior to the year 1844. Here is one of the reasons why they were unprepared for the midnight cry and the first angel's message. Manual labor in connection with education was called by men in these manual training schools "a panacea mighty to heal." The training school for Christian workers which lost that "panacea" became spiritually sick, and ceased to advocate Christian educational reforms. It is called "a missionary impulse," which through manual labor, "made it possible for the very poorest boy or girl to secure an education and thus enlarge his fitness to perform the duties of life."

Oberlin's fruit:—God rewarded this school richly for its adherence to truth and for the product of its labors, in spite of the fact that it was finally compelled to yield. Of Oberlin it is said,

> "Though the very name was so feared and hated, yet there were friends sufficient to desire and solicit more teachers than were to be had. The quality of their work was found to be so excellent that it was wisdom to swallow much prejudice in order to secure the benefit of their instruction. ... One year ... no less than 530 teachers went out for the vocation... Who can measure the benefit bestowed by these great companies of earnest hearted men and women who, for more than a generation, expended their energy upon the children and youth by the tens of thousands... Oberlin is the fruitful mother of colleges.

Olivet College, Tabor College, Benzonia College, Berea College, Fisk University, Talladega College, Atlanta University, Straight University, Emerson Institute, Howard University, and other schools and enterprises absorbed for many years the missionary activity of Oberlin men and women." (*The Story of Oberlin*, p. 320-321).

Their students entered such "foreign fields as Turkey in Europe and in Asia, India, Siam, South America, Haiti, and Burma." (*Oberlin: The Colony and the College*, p. 341).

Students can readily gather from this brief sketch how extended might have been the influence of Oberlin had she remained true to her reform. The words addressed to Seventh-day Adventist educational reformers apply with equal force to the founders of Oberlin.

"Reformers have been handicapped and some have ceased to urge reform. They seem unable to stem the current of doubt and criticism." (*Testimonies for the Church*, Vol. 6, p. 142).

Opposition:—Students will be interested in a few statements showing the decline of these same institutions under the blighting atmosphere of suspicion, criticism, and opposition of the leaders. Oberlin withstood the opposition longer and More successfully than most other schools. The following extract gives the reader a picture of the doubt and criticism brought against Oberlin reforms by the leaders in the Presbyterian and Congregational churches.

"Manual labor, for example, had many friends and admirers, but a large number looked askance at the idea. The student did not need, and could not afford, four hours per day for toil upon the farm or in the shop. Nor was the financial result likely to be of any considerable value, either to him or the institution to which he belonged. [So said the critics.] Thus heads in New England and elsewhere began to shake." (*The Story of Oberlin*, p. 243-247).

Again,

"I have some doubts about a project lately started in this region and which makes no small demands on our regard as an enterprise of benevolence. I refer to Oberlin for which large funds have been received and are collecting. What need is there of another university or college in the woods of Ohio, surrounded by other institutions but a short distance off, still struggling for an existence?... It is said to have manual labor, but so has Hudson. ... Why should students be importuned to leave the institution where they are to go to Oberlin?" (*Ibid.*, p. 247).

Yielding to opposition:—

"After the beginning of the forties, we hear little of manual labor. With the general increase of wealth there was less need of whatever pecuniary value it possessed. The consciences of the good were less scrupulous about seeking exercise outside of useful labor, and the modern gymnasium and athletics soon began to make all-sufficient provision for the physical well-being of the world." (*Ibid.*, p. 231).

Note the year when this decline occurred. Mercer University, referred to above, had this experience:

"In 1844, the manual labor system which had been on trial since the foundation of the Institute in 1833, was abandoned, having proved inefficacious. Several other attempts had been made during the same decade to establish manual labor schools in different places which with one exception had likewise failed." (*Education in Georgia*, p. 65).

Do Seventh-day Adventists grasp the significance of this date? God cannot forever bear with unbelief, half-hearted efforts, and cold, indifferent trifling with divine principles.

"If all who had labored unitedly in the work in 1844 had received the third angel's message and proclaimed it in the power of the Holy Spirit, the Lord would have wrought mightily with their efforts. A flood of light would have been shed upon the world. Years ago the inhabitants of the earth would have been warned, the closing work completed, and Christ would have come for the redemption of his people. It was not the will of God that Israel should wander forty years in the wilderness. He desired to lead them directly to the land of Canaan... In like manner it was not the will of God that the coming Christ should be so long delayed." (*The Great Controversy*, p. 458).

Manual Labor Displaced by Athletics, Sports and Games

No school can successfully maintain manual labor studies in its curriculum on an equality with other studies unless the purpose of God for such a practical training is recognized by both teachers and students. And when the purpose is recognized, the love, interest and enthusiasm generated by an education to do useful things brings more enjoyment and keen pleasure to the student than such substitutes for manual labor as sports and games can ever bring.

> "The physical exercise was marked out by the God of wisdom. Some hours each day should be devoted to useful education in lines of work that will help the students in learning the duties of practical life, which are essential for all our youth. But this has been dropped out, and amusements introduced, which simply give exercise, without being any special blessing in doing good and righteous actions, which is the education and training essential... The time employed in physical exercise, which, step by step, leads on to excess, to intensity in the games and the exercise of the faculties, ought to be used in Christ's lines, and the blessing of God would rest upon them in so doing... Diligent study is essential. ... The influence has been growing among students in their devotion to amusements, to a fascinating, bewitching power, to the counteracting of the influence of the truth upon the human mind and character... What force of powers is put into your games of football and your other inventions after the way of the Gentiles—exercises which bless no one! ... I cannot find an instance in the life of Christ where he devoted time to play and amusement." (Ellen G. White, *Special Testimonies on Education*, pp. 190, 191).

It is easy to determine the system of education in operation in any training school. Students who enjoy games and sports more than useful labor have certainly chosen a system of education that will give them little help in preparing to enter the hard places of the world, or to prepare for the latter rain.

We have already noted that opposition to useful labor in Oberlin brought this change: "The modern gymnasium and athletics soon began to make all sufficient provision for the well-being of the student world." Gradually, "Oberlin introduced modern baseball, football, and athletics in general," (*The Story of Oberlin*, pp. 231, 407), but "the gymnasium made its way slowly at Oberlin, because it seemed to be inconsistent with the manual labor idea." (*Oberlin: The Colony and the College*, p. 262). All this is in harmony with the statement concerning gymnasiums: "They were brought in to supply the want of useful physical training, and have become popular with educational institutions." (*Christian Education*, p. 211).

Before the end, all training schools that are breaking from "the necks of their students worldly yokes," and are bringing their students "into the line of true education," so they may "carry the message of present truth in all its fullness to other countries," ["The Madison School," p. 30] will see that all of these substitutes, such as football, baseball, etc., are replaced by the genuine, useful arts and trades.

STUDENT SELF-GOVERNMENT AND CHRISTIAN DEMOCRACY

Individuality, originality and independence of thought and action on the part of the student are in the end destroyed by the Papal system of education and other systems derived from it. This system is intended by its promoters to destroy these vital elements of character in order to make the individual a willing, blind, obedient servant to the mandates of men. The Papacy can not prosper except as it does destroy these most godlike faculties of man. Individuality, originality and independence of thought and action are developed by Christian education. This system is intended to develop minds capable of being guided by the Holy Spirit, even though that way may be at times diametrically opposed to the rulings of men. They learn to take their orders from the Captain of the Lord's army whose hand is among the wheels of the affairs of men to prevent confusion, anarchy, and disobedience to any organization which is based upon correct principles.

God was preparing a company who could be guided completely by His Spirit in the giving of the midnight cry. Only those trained to take the initiative, to be self-governing, would dare break away at the call of God from the errors and customs of Rome as found in the Protestant churches.

> "The midnight cry was heralded by thousands of believers. Like a tidal wave the movement swept over the land... Fanaticism disappeared before this proclamation like early frost before the rising sun... All were of one heart and of one mind... It caused a weaning of affection from the things of this world, a healing of controversies and animosities, a confession of wrongs... Angels were sent from heaven

to arouse those who had become discouraged, and to prepare them to receive the message... It was not the most talented, but the most humble and devoted who were first to hear and obey the call. Farmers left their crops standing in the fields, merchants laid down their tools, and with tears and rejoicing went out to give the warning. Those who had formerly led in the cause were among the last to join in this movement. The churches in general closed their doors against this message, and a large company of those who received it withdrew their connection... There went with it an impelling power that moved the soul." (*The Great Controversy*, pp. 400-402).

It does not require deep thought to discover the cause of the failure of the educational system of the Protestant denominations to train men and women to participate in the midnight cry. The whole scheme of education of that era, aside from the reform movement which was largely broken down by the pressure of the popular church leaders, was to make men conservative, fearful of leaving the well-trodden paths of action, and of course "the churches in general closed their doors against this message." Protestant teachers and preachers, in harmony with the Papacy, had for years bound the minds of students and church members to creeds both in education and religion, until their adherents were governed by tradition, prejudice, bigotry, and fear of their leaders. They had lost their love and power for self-government. Consequently, God could not lead them by His spirit; their organization was rejected; they had morally fallen; the second angel called them Babylon. On the other hand, a few devoted schools, educational reformers and ministers, had trained a small company to prize the privilege of being governed by the Spirit of God as revealed in His word. They had practiced what they had been taught in self-government, until they were willing to follow the guidance of the Spirit. This shows that true self-government does not mean do-as-you-please; it means that self shall be governed by the Word of God. While this company was cast out of the church organizations, while they left their crops, their tools, and former employments of all kinds to participate in what seemed to those who had not learned self-government to be a fanatical movement, yet from such a company sprang the wonderful Seventh-day Adventist church. And this church is called to set before the world a system of schools, institutions and organizations of self-governing Christians, such as this world has never before seen.

The character capable of carrying the midnight cry had to be developed in the Christian manual training schools, or in the school of the common walks of life. The leader of this movement, William Miller, "the farmer prophet," like Christ and John the Baptist, was educated in the latter. His biographer, a man well qualified to judge the value of the popular educational system of the churches, writes,

> "What now, would have been the effect of what is called a regular course of education? Would it have perverted him, as it has thousands? Or would it have made him instrumental of greater good in the cause of God? Would it have performed its appropriate work, that of disciplining, enlarging, and furnishing the mind, leaving unimpaired by the process its natural energies, its sense of dependence and accountability as to God? Or would it have placed him in the crowded ranks of those who are content to share in the honor of repeating the twaddle, true or false, which passes for truth in the school or sect which has made them what they are? We think it would have been difficult to pervert him; but where so many who have been regarded as highly promising have been marred by the operation, he would have been in great danger. He might have become externally a better subject for the artist; *but we doubt if he would have been a better subject to be used as an instrument of Providence.* There are those who survive the regular course uninjured; there are those who are benefited by it, so far as to be raised to a level with people of ordinary capacity, which they never could attain without special aid. And there is a third class, who are a stereotype representation of what the course makes them; if they raise a fellowman out of the mire, they never get him nearer to heaven than the school where they were educated. Whatever might have been the result of any established course of education in the case of William Miller, such a course was beyond his reach; he was deprived of the benefit, he has escaped the perversion." (James S. White, *Sketches of the Christian Life and Public Labors of William Miller*, p. 15-16).

This is that William Miller, "the farmer prophet," who later brought the first angel's message to Oberlin. The futility of depending upon men who have not been trained to self-government has been seen in the midnight cry experience. Every Seventh-day Adventist is approaching his final test, just as the Protestant churches approached theirs in 1844. Ours will come with the loud cry, the latter rain. Those who lack training for self-government, those not able to depend upon their own efforts for support, who are not making the Bible the basis of study, and physiology the basis of every educational effort; all who, in other words, "do not understand the true science of education" will have no part in the kingdom of God or in the loud cry.

Character needed for the loud cry is similar to that of the midnight cry:—

> "The message of the third angel will be proclaimed. As the time comes for it to be given with the greatest power, the Lord will work through humble instruments, leading the minds of those who consecrate themselves to His service. The laborers will be qualified rather by the unction of His Spirit than by the training of literary institutions. Men of faith and of prayer will be constrained to go forth with holy zeal proclaiming the words which God gives them." (*The Great Controversy*, p. 606).

The Jesuit schools taught their students blind obedience. The student was not required to go to God for wisdom regarding his conduct. His teacher assumed that responsibility. True self-government, which may be defined as bringing one's conduct into harmony with God's principles as expressed in His Word, was absolutely neglected. The terrible effects of the Papal system of school discipline has been seen during the first angel's message. Those students who blindly followed teachers rather than God's principles were bound by customs, traditions, organizations and leaders at a time when the Spirit of God was calling them to follow the truth. As a preparation for the loud cry, we are told,

> "The plan of the schools we shall establish in these closing years of the work is to be of an entirely different order from those we have instituted." ("The Madison School," p. 28).

> "The object of discipline is the training of the child for self-government." (Ellen G. White, *Education*, p. 287).

> "Having never learned to govern himself, the youth recognizes no restraint except the requirement of parents or teacher. This removed, he knows not how to use his liberty, and often gives himself up to indulgence that proves his ruin." (*Ibid.*, p. 288).

> "They should not be led to feel that they cannot go out or come in without being watched." (*Ibid.*, p. 289).

"Lead the youth to feel that they are trusted, and there are few who will not seek to prove themselves worthy of the trust... It is better to request than to command; the one thus addressed has opportunity to prove himself loyal to right principles. His obedience is the result of choice rather than compulsion. The rules governing the schoolroom should, so far as possible, represent the voice of the school... Thus he will feel a responsibility to see that the rules which he himself has helped to frame are obeyed. Rules should be few and well considered; and when once made, they should be enforced." (*Ibid.*, p. 290).

"Those who desire to control others must first control themselves." (Ellen G. White, *Education*, p. 292).

"Co-operation should be the spirit of the school room, the law of its life... Let the older assist the younger; the strong the weak. This will encourage self-respect and a desire to be useful." (*Ibid.*, p. 285).

Jefferson, the father of democracy, knowing that self-government was not taught in the schools of his day, and that democracy cannot exist in the State unless its principles are first taught and practiced in the school, introduced this principle into the University of Virginia.

"It is very generally known that at the University of Virginia exists a remarkable system of student self-government, by which a high morale and a manly tone of self-reliance have been successfully maintained." (*Thomas Jefferson and the University of Virginia*, p. 94).

Self-government is contrasted with what is called "professorial espionage."

"Self-government established a frank and kindly spirit of cooperation between master and pupil. It repressed all dishonorable practices of cheating in recitations and examinations, and promoted a spirit of independence and self-respect." (*Idem*).

Oberlin found it necessary, in the training of the right kind of missionaries, to develop a system of self-government. In Oberlin

"the democratic feeling, the spirit of equality, the absence of classes and casts based upon mere artificial distinctions, is almost as marked in the institution as in the village... The Faculty ... never sought to lord it over the students as being themselves superior, nor have insisted upon a particular show of homage, reverence, or respect even... They played instead the role of elder brothers to their pupils." (*The Story of Oberlin*, p. 398).

Titles were unknown, and students addressed their teachers as "Brother Finney," or "Brother Mahan".

> "Self-rule was the ideal. The assembled youth were to learn how to use freedom by being left free. A right public sentiment was to be the controlling force." (*Ibid.*, p. 409).

> "Each individual has full liberty to make the most of himself, and stands for just what he is actually worth in heart or brain. Class yells and class colors have come in of late, occasionally class hats, canes, and the like, at rare intervals the class robe, but with the consensus of judgment and taste heavily against any wide departure from fashions of dress in vogue elsewhere in good society." (*The Story of Oberlin*, p. 399).

In oberlin,

> "the regulations are few. No strict personal surveillance was ever undertaken. The student has been thrown greatly on his own responsibility, with the understanding that his continual enjoyment of the privileges of the school must depend upon his satisfactory deportment... No monitorial system has ever been adopted. Each young man reports weekly in writing to the professor in charge, his success or failure in attendance upon prescribed duties. The young women report to the lady principal." (*Oberlin: The Colony and the College*, pp. 263-265).

This sounds very much like the following:

> "The youth must be impressed with the idea that they are trusted... If pupils receive the impression that they cannot go out or come in, sit at the table, or be anywhere, even in their rooms, except they are watched, a critical eye is upon them, to criticise and report, it will have the influence to demoralize, and pastime will have no pleasure in it. This knowledge of a continual oversight is more than a parental guardianship, and far worse... This constant watchfulness is not natural, and produces evils that it is seeking to avoid." (*Christian Education*, p. 46).

Horace Mann on self-government:—In those days when the Protestant denominations were settling their eternal destiny, when they were determining whether they would hear the world-wide judgment message, and themselves be prepared for the midnight cry, such men as Horace Mann wrote, "One of the highest and most valuable objects to which the influences of a school can be made conducive, consists in training our children to be self-governing." Mr. Mann had the following experience in dealing with students. He gave the young men to understand "that he looked to them to be their own police: and when a tutor, who had resided in a gentlemen's dormitory to keep order, was exchanged for a lady teacher, he appealed to the senior class, one day after chapel service, to know if they were not sufficiently strong in moral force to take care of the building without such supervision. They rose to their feet simultaneously, accepted the trust joyfully and confidently, kept the promise well, and transmitted its spirit to their successors." (*Life and Works of Horace Mann*, vol. 1, p. 438).

Mr. Mann, however, was always on the alert to assist these self-governing students by a word of caution, or by forewarning them of impending trouble. "It was Mr. Mann's pride and delight ever after to walk through the gentlemen's hall at any hour of the day or night, and to take visitors with him to convince them that a true spirit of honor and fidelity could be evoked from the young" in matters of self-government. At one time he wrote,

"Our dormitory, nearly filled with male students, has no tutor or proctor or overseer. In study-hours, it is as quiet as your house. We have no rowdyism, no drinking of intoxicating liquors, no gambling or card-playing; and we have nearly succeeded... in exorcising profanity and tobacco." (*Ibid.*, p. 515).

"Go to the ant, thou sluggard;
Consider her ways, and be wise;
Which having no guide, overseer, or ruler,
Provideth her meat in the summer,
And gathereth her food in the harvest."
Proverbs 6:6-8.

TRAINING MISSIONARIES TO BE SELF-SUPPORTING — A LAYMEN'S MISSIONARY MOVEMENT

It was the divine plan that the midnight cry and the third angel's message should be carried to every nation, kindred, tongue and people. God wanted an army trained to carry forth this practical religion to a world which had been educated away from the gospel order by the pagan and Papal systems of education.

We have seen that Christian education, as developed by the educational reformers in every Protestant denomination, made possible a mighty laymen's movement. We can understand how these self-supporting missionaries could quickly carry the message to the world. It was Satan's studied effort to thwart this self-supporting laymen's movement. He accomplished his desired results by exalting worldly literature to a place above the Bible; by consuming practically all the student's time in mental effort, and leading him to depreciate the practical in education; by leading to a gradual substitution of athletics, sports and games for manual labor. Satan is endeavoring to deceive the very elect, the remnant church.

The Protestant denominations could not "carry the message of present truth in all its fullness to other countries," because they did not "first break every yoke" of worldly education; they did not "come into the line of true education;" they did not educate to "prepare a people" to "understand the message, and then give the message to the world." ("The Madison School," p. 28).

Self-supporting students and teachers:—

"The pupils of these schools [of the prophets] sustained themselves by their own labor in tilling the soil or in some mechanical employment... Many of the religious teachers supported themselves by manual labor." (*Christian Education*, p. 61).

"Schools are to be established away from the cities, where the youth can learn to cultivate the soil and thus help to make themselves and the school self-supporting... Let means be gathered for the establishment of such schools." (*Testimonies for the Church*, Vol. 7, p. 232).

"The presentation in our schools should not now be as it has been in the past in introducing many things as essential that are only of minor importance." (Ellen G. White, "Words of Encouragement to Self-supporting Workers," *Pamphlet 113*, p. 20 [Jan. 9, 1909]).

"Your school is to be an example of how Bible study, general education, physical education, and sanitarium work may be combined in many smaller schools that will be established in simplicity in many places." (Ellen G. White, *The Spalding and Magan Collection*, p. 420 [Jan. 6, 1908]).

"We need schools that will be self-supporting, and this can be if teachers and students will be helpful, industrious, and economical... Sacrifices must be made on every hand." ("Words of Encouragement to Self-supporting Workers," p. 28 [Jan. 24, 1907]).

Work for the self-supporting laymen:—

"The time is soon coming when God's people, because of persecution, will be scattered in many countries. Those who have received as all-round education will have a great advantage wherever they are." (Ellen G. White, "An Appeal for the Madison School," *Pamphlet 119*, p. 2).

The apostle Paul

"illustrated in a practical way what might be done by consecrated laymen in many places... There is a large field open before the self-supporting gospel worker... From heaven he receives his commission and to heaven he looks for his recompense when the work entrusted to him is done." (Ellen G. White, *The Acts of the Apostles*, pp. 355-356).

Many educational reformers prior to 1844 were impressed by the Spirit of God to give a practical education in order that their students might be free to carry the truth to any field to which God might call. These reformers saw that the educational system in vogue in the Protestant churches was totally inadequate to prepare a missionary to dare to carry an unpopular truth contrary to the will of the leaders in those denominations.

"Professor Finney of Oberlin College said, 'We have had the fact before our minds, that, in general, the Protestant churches of our country, as such, were either apathetic or hostile to nearly all the moral reforms of the age... the *churches generally are becoming sadly degenerate*. They have gone very far from the Lord, and He has withdrawn Himself from them.'" (*The Great Controversy*, p. 377).

"The churches generally did not accept the warning. Their ministers ... had failed to learn the truth either from the testimony of the prophets or from the signs of the times... The fact that the message was, to a great extent, preached by laymen, was urged as an instrument against it... Multitudes, trusting implicitly to their pastors, refused to listen to the warning." (*Ibid.*, p. 380).

Hundreds of self-supporting missionaries were sent out by this same President Finney of Oberlin who

"laid down the somewhat ultra and startling dictum that nobody was fit to be a missionary who was not willing, with but an ear of corn in his pocket, to start for the Rocky Mountains." (*The Story of Oberlin*, p. 238).

This was the spirit of faith and daring awakened in the hearts of students who were taught to make their way from the soil.

The American Educational Society was the educational department of the Congregational denomination, and its work was to superintend all the educational institutions of that denomination. Oberlin was established by godly men in the Congregational church who desired to make their school a means of training Congregational missionaries.

> "Some of the candidates for the ministry made application to that organization for financial help ... which step the trustees refused to countenance, but afterward, though grudgingly and unhandsomely allowed... Oberlin entered into a prolonged tilt with the American Educational Society of which the provoking cause was contained in certain pet ideas of the founders, notably, the one with regard to self-support to be made easily possible through the sovereign virtues of manual labor." (*Ibid.*, pp. 250, 249).

Oberlin's effort to train self-supporting missionaries, was attacked by Hudson College, a Congregational school which attempted to injure the influence of Oberlin in the denomination. "Here was too good an opportunity for Hudson to miss." In January, 1837, came this unjust criticism from Hudson,

> "When Oberlin started it was said that students would support themselves, thus not needing help. It operated against the Educational Society, and many refused to contribute, so when Oberlin became convinced that its scheme was visionary, and sought aid for students, the Board asked them to say frankly that Oberlin was not self-supporting, in order to disabuse the public of that notion. This has not been done... We are sorry they do not say right out 'We are not self-supporting.' So now it seems that Oberlin students cannot earn any more than others and need as much help. Thus Oberlin manual labor is no better than it is elsewhere." (*Ibid.*, p. 250).

Oberlin was not always a favorite with sister institutions, and "was made to appear as a troubler in Israel, an Ishmaelite. Lane and Hudson had a grievance. Here was a shameless trespasser, a poacher upon their preserves." (*Ibid.*, p. 150). This was felt because of the "wholesale exodus of students who had flocked to Mr. Shipherd's school." The faculties of Lane and Hudson felt that "in all things, while Oberlin was radical, they were conservative. Yes, and Oberlin was overrun with students." and this in spite of the fact that "Oberlin wrought with all her might to restore to the churches the purely democratic polity of New England. Therefore, by a multitude of the good, Oberlin was abhorred and cast out as vile." "Oberlin is said to be manual labor, but so is Hudson. It is said that the students come from the east, but why should they come away from the excellent, long-tried, richly endowed, and well officered institutions in the older states to get an education in a meager and poorly furnished institute in the wilds of Ohio? Why should students be importuned to leave institutions where they are to go to Oberlin, as I understand has been extensively the case in this region?" (*Ibid.*, p. 247). So said Oberlin's critics.

The managers of Oberlin felt keenly these thrusts from their own brethren who occupied leading positions. The accusations were not true. Oberlin was sending hundreds of self-supporting missionaries to the Indians, the mountaineers of the South, to the freedmen, and to other needy fields. It aroused President Mahan to reply,

> "'We do not feel called upon to say or do anything. We do not much care whether the Society aids our students or not. If we want help we can get it.' Thus stigmatized and cast out, what could Oberlin and her friends do but organize an educational society of their own? ... [Oberlin] was charged far and wide with the sin of schism, with being a foe to Christian union, with tugging with might and main to overthrow the ecclesiastical *status quo*... It was presently Oberlin's lot to be cast out as vile, and but for the existence of the Association and other subordinate bodies affiliated with it, Oberlin's students would have been unable to secure either license or ordination." (*Ibid.*, pp. 251, 252).

In 1839, the Congregational church put this query in their church paper regarding Oberlin:

> "Shall young men go there expecting to get a thorough, classical, and theological education? Will such be received by the churches as pastors or missionaries? Is there any obligation to aid Oberlin as now constituted?" (*Ibid.*, p. 254).

In 1840, two Oberlin students

> "asked to be licensed, and their case was referred to a committee, which without the least questioning, simply asked if they believed in the doctrines taught at Oberlin and their way of doing things.

Declining to answer such an inquiry, it was finally changed to this, 'Do you believe on the whole, that Oberlin is a good institution, or is it a curse to the world?' They then confessed that they thought it was good, and also believed the committee would think so too if they would spend a week there." (*Ibid.*, pp. 254, 255).

The license was refused these Oberlin students.

The Congregational Conference then took this action toward Oberlin, "We deem it inexpedient for our churches to employ ministers known to cherish Oberlin ideas." (*Ibid.*, pp. 255, 256). In 1841, this question was raised by the Conference of Ohio, "Will baptism pass muster as valid if administered by an Oberlin man?" (*Ibid.*, p. 256). The question was referred to a committee which reported,

> "Oberlin ideas are exceedingly dangerous and corrupting, and these preachers should not be received by the churches as orthodox ministers, nor should their members be admitted to the communion."

> "In 1944, the General Conference of New York condemned the heresy and censured the Genessee Conference for winking at it... The American Board discharged two noble missionaries, Bradley and Casswell in Siam for the same reason... The Cleveland convention was held this year, but the conference with which the Oberlin church was connected was not invited to a share in its deliberations. Mr. Finney and President Mahan were present, but a motion that they be invited to sit as corresponding members was voted down, by a considerable majority as one delegate testifies. But much of the time was spent in denouncing Oberlin, and the chief object of the convention seemed to be to destroy its influence, and exclude it from the pale of orthodoxy." (*Ibid.*, pp. 256, 257).

American Missionary Association formed:—

> "When Oberlin men would go as missionaries to the Northwest, it became necessary to bring into being, the Western Evangelical Missionary Society to send and support them, and when they undertook work in behalf of the negroes whether in Ohio, Canada or the West Indies or Africa, other organizations were required, which, in 1846, were united in the American Missionary Association, which also for years, with its operations, covered the home as well as the foreign field... The evil feeling which was very prevalent and widely extended found frequent expression in language like this: A delegate in the Cleveland Convention said, 'The influence of Oberlin was worse than that of Roman Catholicism.' The President of the Mich-

igan University publicly avowed the belief that 'Oberlin theology was almost devilish.' Still another brother said, 'Brethren, I hate Oberlin almost as badly as I hate slavery, and you know I hate slavery as I hate the devil." (*Ibid.*, pp. 257, 258).

When Oberlin students applied to the American Educational Society to be sent as missionaries to the Indians, the Society replied, "We cannot. You are good men, and we wish you well, but it will not do." At another time, "the Board instructed one of its missionaries to be careful how he associated with Oberlin men on terms of too great intimacy, lest they be poisoned by their influence." An Oberlin student had applied for a position as minister in a Congregational church. The examining board asked, "If installed, will you allow President Mahan or Professor Finney of Oberlin to preach in your pulpit? And as he replied that he would, a half day was consumed in considering if they should proceed with the examination. When one spoke of the Oberlin brethren, another said, 'They are not brethren, they are aliens,' and almost the entire body was in sympathy with this statement." (*Ibid.*, pp. 249, 265).

Oberlin was being baptized with fire. These experiences were taken, in the most part, in a kindly spirit. They attended to their own business, and sent out a constant stream of live, enthusiastic, successful, soul-saving missionaries. They were beginning to appreciate the truth of this wonderful statement concerning Christian education:

> "When we reach the standard that the Lord would have us reach, worldlings will regard Seventh-day Adventists as odd, singular, straight-laced extremists." (Ellen G. White, *Review and Herald*, Jan. 9, 1894).

> "I want you to guard one point; do not be easily disturbed by what others may say. Know that you are right, and then go ahead... Do not be troubled by the opinions of those who talk for the sake of talking." (Ellen G. White, *Pamphlet 158*, p. 13 [July 18, 1892]).

Remember that Mrs. E. G. White refers to Oberlin history when the institution was passing through these experiences by saying,

> "The churches generally are becoming sadly degenerate. They have gone very far from the Lord, and He has withdrawn Himself from them." (*The Great Controversy*, p. 377).

Had Oberlin yielded to the demands of the church; had she not endeavored to obey God even under difficulties, she would never have accomplished what she did. For it was in the face of these experiences that she succeeded in placing more missionaries among the freedmen than all other American colleges combined. The spirit of the Lord helped Oberlin teachers to recognize under the conditions of that time, the principle in the following statement:

> "It is not the Lord's will that the work in the South shall be confined to the set, regular lines. It has been found impossible to confine the work to these lines, and gain success. Workers daily filled with zeal and wisdom from on high must work as they are guided by the Lord, waiting not to receive their commission from men." (Ellen G. White, *The Southern Watchman*, 15 de dezembro de 1903, par. 14).

A manual labor student of Oberlin becomes president:—The experience of Professor James H. Fairchild, who was connected with Oberlin for over sixty years, first as a student and then as a teacher, bears witness to the fact that Oberlin did make it possible for students to be self-supporting. Professor Fairchild writes, "A very obvious reason for choosing this institution was my financial limitations." Speaking of himself at seventeen, he says,

> "My parents could spare me from the farm, but could not furnish money even for tuition. Oberlin was a manual labor school, and my brother and myself, taking the first course together, were manual labor students. On our first arrival we were put in charge of the lath-sawing in the mill, four hours a day, five cents an hour. This provided for our expenses the first year. The next and following years we worked as carpenters and joiners on the college buildings and the homes in the colony. By such labor, re-enforced by the wages of teaching in vacation, we earned our way through the entire course, without any sense of want or weariness, or any hindrance to our studies, or to our general preparation for the work of life." (*The Story of Oberlin*, p. 290).

This young man was a theological student, and with others from his class went out among the churches as a self-supporting minister. This was the preparation he received which fitted him to occupy a place first as instructor in Oberlin, and later as President of the institution with which he spent his life.

Salary:—The character of the teachers that give students an inspiration to self-supporting work is thus described in the person of an Oberlin professor:

"His piety is more like the divine Teacher's than usual; he labors with his might to do good in school and out; his education, though not collegiate, is sufficiently extensive; he is a manual labor man; he does not teach for money *but to do good; he is deeply interested in the West.*" (*Ibid.*, p. 96).

Concerning the wages of this man, a member of the Board wrote,

"I advise that you offer him $400.00 with the use of a dwelling-house and a few acres of land, hay for his horse and two cows, and his wood." (*Idem*).

Of the founders of Oberlin it is said,

"These unselfish and self-denying souls offered themselves to the institution without salary for five years." (*Ibid.*, p. 269).

Oberlin was able to be self-supporting, partly because she reduced the size of her faculty by utilizing student teachers, and partly because the members of her faculty were willing to sacrifice in the matter of wages.

The students who sought an education in such an institution were as strongly characteristic as the teachers. Of Oberlin students it is said,

"With their own muscle, they were working their way into the ministry. Most were of comparatively mature years, while some were past thirty... It was a noble class of young men, uncommonly strong, a little uncivilized, entirely radical, and terribly in earnest." (*Ibid.*, p. 132).

Self-supporting missionaries:—These schools which were wrestling with the problems of true education, were all of them, training missionaries and evangelists. They held a definite object before their students, a life work which called for self-sacrifice and devotion. This in itself put zeal and life into the work of teachers and students. The world was approaching one of the most momentous years in its history. The judgment message was due. Intensity was taking hold of men in every station of life. Students in these schools were alive to the great social questions of the day, and instead of spending their time and energy in the study of dead classics, and other impractical subjects which have little or no value in the training of Christian workers, they were dealing with live problems which called for activity as well as thought. For instance, Oberlin students were devoting themselves to mission work among the Indians. They were educating the colored people; they were sending workers into the mountain districts of the South, and even into the islands of the sea.

"Every long vacation numbers of [Oberlin] students, made their way to southern Ohio, wherever these poor [colored] were gathered, and lavished upon them sympathy and compassion, receiving only their bare living. In 1836, Hiram Wilson, a Lane student, proceeded to upper Canada to work among the twenty thousand freedmen who had fled from slavery to that place of refuge. They were in deepest poverty and ignorance. To the task of Christianizing and educating them, he devoted his whole life. At the end of two years fourteen teachers from Oberlin were assisting him. In 1840 no less than thirty-nine were teaching colored schools in Ohio, half of them young women, receiving their board only, and as many more in Canada." (*Ibid.*, pp. 322, 323).

It was such experiences that prepared these young people to do a most efficient work for the freedmen.

Much of this work was on a self-supporting basis.

"The great body of young men who went out from Oberlin to preach in the early days, went as home missionaries—with this exception, that they looked to no society to aid the churches in paying their salaries. It was not difficult to find needy churches to welcome them... Such was the prevalent ignorance and misapprehension in regard to Oberlin, that the most they could look for was the privilege of working in some needy field without molestation. Each man was obliged to find a place for himself, and slowly secure recognition. Under these conditions. Oberlin men found their work and waited for a brighter day." (*Ibid.*, pp. 323, 324).

Missionaries to Cuba:—In 1836 a student seeking a warm climate for health's sake, went to Cuba.

"Being a skilled mechanic he found self-support easy, and while there conceived the idea of a mission to the blacks of Jamaica to be carried on independent of any outside assistance." (*Ibid.*, p. 325).

One of the missions started in Cuba was named Oberlin.

"For fifteen Years the call for recruits continued, and was responded to, until in all, thirty-six had gone forward. For several years, these much enduring men and women, aside from the pittance which the ex-slaves could bestow, depended almost wholly upon the labor of their own hands. In addition, they built their own dwellings as well as chapels and school houses." (*Idem*).

Oberlin was training men to proclaim an unpopular message, and these experiences were a part of their training.

"A year or two of self-denying and efficient labor with some needy church without aid, was the usual probation to a recognized ministerial standing. Theological students going out to preach found no missionary society to guide them to open doors, and to secure them compensation for the service. They went where preaching seemed to be needed, and often returned as empty handed as they went, except for the friendship and gratitude of those to whom they carried the work of the gospel." (*Ibid.*, p. 324).

One today might wonder how they lived, but the writer goes on to say,

"They were manual labor students and could make their way in Oberlin another year. The situation had its advantages. The Oberlin man secured a theological standing of its own—a birth-right of liberty. This freedom may have come at a heavy price, but it was worth the having." (*Idem*).

This is an illustration of the great principle given us:

"Culture on all points of practical life will make our youth useful after they shall leave school to go to foreign countries. They will not then have to depend upon the people to whom they go to cook and sew for them, or build their habitations. They will be much more influential if they show that they can educate the ignorant how to labor with the best methods, and to produce the best results... A much smaller fund will be required to sustain such missionaries... And wherever they may go, all that they have gained in this line will give them standing room." (*The Spalding and Magan Collection*, p. 50).

Oberlin helps students find their life work:—

"[Oberlin] never stood so exclusively as did the old-fashioned colleges for a culture purely scholastic in its nature for book learning. More emphasis was laid upon the practical side. Knowledge was good through its uses... Oberlin has always been impressed by the fact that what the world most needs is character, men and women of genuine worth and power whose aims are unselfish and noble, who count service a delight... [The teachers] were overflowing with stimulus to thought and enthusiasm... The superficial, the namby-pamby, has been held in contempt... The mightiest questions were daily brought up for discussion." (*The Story of Oberlin*, pp. 399, 400).

"[Oberlin] was composed wholly of elect persons, who came on a mission, with a burden, a definite purpose... One of the early graduates used to tell how, as he bade the class goodbye when he had completed his course in an eastern academy, the principal commiserated them upon the fact that they had been born so late in history that all the really important tasks had been performed, so that nothing remained for them but the ignoble work of helping to keep the wheels of progress moving along in the old ruts! But entering the little clearing in the forest [Oberlin] he soon discovered that the universal conviction there was that a multitude of mighty questions were yet calling for solution; that the world's redemption was only just fairly begun." (*Ibid.*, p. 298).

Teachers are more important than expensive equipment to inspire students.

"Among Oberlin's leaders were men of remarkable power who uttered their convictions in such a masterful fashion as to make them deeply felt far and wide. Moreover, these men were of an intensely practical make. Thought, investigation, opinion found their fitting goal only in volition and action. Their definition of Christianity was broad enough to include every matter connected with human welfare. Every year they arouse and inspired hundreds of most impressible minds and hearts." (*Idem*).

"Say not, 'We cannot afford to work in a sparsely settled field, and largely in a self-supporting way...' God desires that every man shall stand in his lot and in his place and not feel as if the work was too hard." ("Words of Encouragement to Self-supporting workers," pp. 12, 15).

Oberlin's influence felt:—The historian gives the effect of such training in the following words:

"It would be hard to overestimate the part in this work which was taken by Oberlin missionaries. Remember that they numbered hundreds at an early day, and soon exceeded thousands... They scattered westward, eastward, and even southward, always pushing, debating inquiring, agitating. It bubbled from their lips as naturally as their breath, and they could not refrain from it... Oberlin is peculiar among all the learned institutions of the land in having so large a constituency of temporary students inculcated with her spirit, but not having her diploma; the bone and sinew of the country wherever they are; active and influential in their modest spheres, and always ready to second the efforts and sustain the work of her more authoritative representatives whenever they appear... There is hardly a township west of the Alleghenies and north of the central line of Ohio, in which the influence of Oberlin men and Oberlin opinions cannot be specifically identified and traced. It was the propaganda of a school of thought and action having distinct characteristics." (*The Story of Oberlin*, pp. 314, 315).

Perhaps there is no other one experience that better illustrates the great power of Oberlin people, and their daring in taking the initiative against popular opinion, than their attitude toward the slavery question, and the freedmen. When we see the work done along this line, we can better appreciate the value of Oberlin's system of education along the lines of Bible study, the discarding of injurious literature, her indifference to school honors, her manual training, self-government and self-support. Without such training, it would have been difficult for Oberlin students to pursue the course they did on the slavery question. It brought them in conflict with the laws of the land, but the students obeyed the laws of God rather than the laws of men. The following statement was addressed by a civil judge to an Oberlin man who was on trial for assisting a slave to escape:

> "A man of your intelligence must know that if the standard of right is placed above and against the laws of the land, those who stand up for it are anything else than good citizens and good Christians... His conduct is as criminal as his example is dangerous. (*Oberlin: The Colony and the College*, p. 125).

Desire to reform aroused by correlation:—The secret of the success of Oberlin teachers in arousing students to take a stand on this debated question, and put themselves where they became leaders in a practical movement to arouse the minds of the people to the terrible wickedness of slavery as an institution, lay in the fact that Oberlin did not conduct her class work and her lectures along the regular stereotype lines of the schools about them. On the contrary, Oberlin on every occasion correlated this subject with the daily work in the classroom. One of Oberlin's enemies understood this secret at the time, and wrote,

> "With arithmetic is taught the computation of the number of slaves and their value per head; with geography, territorial lines and those localities of slave territory supposed to be favorable to emancipation; with history, the chronicles of the peculiar institution; with ethics and philosophy, the higher law and resistance to federal enactments. Hence, the graduates of Oberlin are masters of art in abolitionism, and with the acquirement of their degrees are prepared to go a degree or two further if occasion requires... They imagine that they are doing God's service. There may be some excuse for them (the students) but there is none for their instructors. We doubt if there is for either. So

long as Oberlin flourishes and educates 1250 students per annum, male and female abolitionists will continue to multiply." (*The Story of Oberlin*, p. 265).

It has always been God's plan as illustrated by the schools of the prophets, that the Christian school should be the nursery in which reformers are born and reared reformers who would go forth from the school burning with practical zeal and enthusiasm to take their places as leaders in these reforms. He intends that the teachers shall be leaders in reform, and possessed of sufficient ingenuity and adaptability to make a vital connection between every lesson and reforms. It was this method that made Wittenberg the center of the 16th century Reformation.

Fear to accept and act reforms—a mark of Papal system of education:—It has ever been the policy of the Papacy to sterilize the brains of teachers so that they cannot be impregnated with reform ideas. The Papal system of education makes them content to repeat set lessons to their students, as they themselves learned them in school, with no thought of making practical application. The students, in turn, go out to teach others the same rote they have learned, and thus the endless treadmill goes on, ever learning, but never getting anywhere.

Macaulay thus describes this system:

> "The ancient philosophy was a treadmill not a path. It was made up of revolving questions of controversies which were always beginning again. It was a contrivance for having much exertion and no progress... The human mind, accordingly, instead of marching, merely marked time. It took as much trouble as would have sufficed to carry it forward, and yet remained on the same spot. There was no accumulation of truth... There had been plenty of plowing, harrowing, reaping, threshing. But the garners contained only smut and stubble." ("Essay on Francis Bacon", *The Edinburgh Review*, pp. 344, 345).

Any school which, like Oberlin, has power to arouse its students to carry out a reform for which God is calling, must expect to meet with the same bitter opposition from those who are content with the mere form of Christian education without the power of the Spirit. These are wells without water; clouds without rain, words without ideas, lamps without oil.

Opposition arouses investigation leading to friendship:—In the days when Thomas Jefferson was meeting with the keenest criticism because of the reforms in education which he advocated, he found friends for his reforms even in the more conservative schools. For instance, Professor George Ticknor, a member of the Harvard faculty, made a careful study of Jefferson's views of education. He surprised his friends by traveling six hundred miles by stage-coach and the slow conveyance of that period, and endured "with patience the annoyance of bad roads and the discomfort of bad inns. ... What was he thinking of in such a long journey southward? ... He was going to see Jefferson's new university 'fairly opened'", and of it he wrote, that "he found 'the system' 'more practical' than he had feared. He found 'an experiment worth trying.'" (*Thomas Jefferson and the University of Virginia*, p. 129).

Oberlin's attendance a mystery:—We have seen the jealousy and critical attitude of many of the leaders toward Oberlin. It was difficult for Oberlin to bear the irritation that was so constantly kept up, but God looked with pleasure upon the manner with which Oberlin met this persecution.

> "For the most part, little pains have been taken to forge or wield weapons of defense. She had gone forward patiently and persistently, minding her own business and doing her own work in her own way, assured that full vindication would eventually come. For one thing, all along she had the comfort of knowing that devoted and admiring friends were not wanting, and could see that a phenomenal success at many points had been achieved. With students of both sexes, she was fairly flooded. This same surprising and unprecedented growth in spite of extreme poverty, in spite of some serious errors and blunders, in spite of hosts of foes whose united strength seemed overwhelming, constituted a mystery which the most sapient of her calumniators was unable to solve. One of these expressed the perplexing fact to Mr. Finney something like this: 'It has always been understood that no institution could prosper or achieve success without having the sympathy and cooperation of both churches and ministers. In your case the multitude of these have either stood aloof, or have been actively hostile; and yet you secure students, teachers, buildings, and endowments far beyond the most fortunate of your neighbors. We cannot understand it at all.'" (*The Story of Oberlin*, p. 263).

"No educational institution can place itself in opposition to the errors and corruptions of this degenerate age without receiving threats and insults. But time will place such an institution upon an elevated platform having the assurance of God that they have acted right." (Ellen G. White, *General Conference Bulletin*, 1901, p. 454).

SELECTING AND TRAINING TEACHERS

Undoubtedly, more failures have come to educational reforms and to schools, through the inability of the founders to select teachers in sympathy with Christian education, and who have the ability to teach the essential branches as directed by the angels who wait to co-operate in the teaching of every class, than through any other one weakness. Teachers have been employed in Christian schools "who could pass well in a worldly institution of learning," but who could not follow the divine pattern as revealed to the founders. For this reason, many schools, established by reformers, soon patterned after the popular schools.

> "God has revealed to me that we are in positive danger of bringing into our educational work the customs and fashions that prevail in schools of the world." ("The Madison School," p. 28).

> "Let not managers, teachers, or helpers swing back in their old customary ways of letting their influence negative the very plans the Lord has presented as the best plan for the physical, mental, and moral education of our youth. The Lord calls for steps in advance." (*The Spalding and Magan Collection*, p. 204 [Dec. 27, 1901]).

Oberlin was terribly pressed by her own brethren who were ignorant of the nature and value of the educational light God had so generously revealed to her. But severe as was the criticism and pressure from the outside, Oberlin might carry out God's plan in the preparation of an army of missionaries to give the midnight cry, had not some of her teachers continued to cling to the principles and methods of worldly schools. The germ that finally caused her to stagger in her course was planted in her vitals by members of her own faculty. One example of the many that might be given is sufficient to make this matter clear.

> "Professor J. P. Cowles never looked with favor upon such dietetic vagaries; he did not scruple to ridicule and otherwise oppose them, and as he himself states, furnished pepper boxes, and kept the tables

supplied with pepper for months, although eventually the prudential committee took them away." (*The Story of Oberlin*, p. 422).

The influence of this teacher with some others who were opposed to President Finney's position on pepper and other condiments, tea, coffee, flesh foods, etc., and who failed to realize this health reform as an entering wedge, is thus stated,

> "Under the pressure of this panic, they rushed with precipitous and confused haste back to their flesh pots; and here, under the exhilarating influence of fresh infusions of the Chinese shrub, the Mocha bean, with the riotous eating of swine's flesh, and drinking the broth of abominable things, they succeeded in arresting a necessary renovating work." (*Ibid.*, p. 424).

Opposition from without, trying; from within, serious:—The nagging, the sneers, and the falsehoods of those outside Oberlin's walls, who were out of sympathy with her reforms, were unpleasant and serious obstacles, but the opposition of certain teachers who were continually undermining the love and respect of students for health reform was fatal to progress in all reform. In yielding on health reform, Oberlin began to relinquish her reforms one by one until she was unable to meet the test in 1844. Thus Oberlin failed in the great mission to which she was called by the First Angel, because some of her teachers were not in sympathy with Christian education. On those reforms where the faculty agreed, Oberlin made a world-wide record.

Jefferson's school finally lost out in its reforms because he was unwise enough to select a number of members for the faculty of the University of Virginia from the universities of Europe. Wise as was Jefferson on many great questions, he was weak on this point, and it is said that

> "Washington demurred; he doubted the expediency of importing a body of foreign professors who would be inclined to bring from the European schools ideas at variance with the principles of democracy," which Jefferson wanted to make basic in his school. (*Thomas Jefferson and the University of Virginia*, p. 45).

It was for this same reason that the staunch Puritan reformers lost their hold on those Principles that would have prepared their descendants for the midnight cry. They established a number of schools, such as Harvard and Yale, that for years were recognized as Bible schools, but they were under the influence of teachers who, as we have learned, brought to them the Papal principles of education from Oxford, Eton, and other European schools, and this finally destroyed the desire for reform. If there is one thing above another that Seventh-day Adventists have been cautioned about, it is this point. Wrecks of Christian education have been strewn all along the way, just because teachers have opposed reforms as did that Oberlin teacher who insisted on putting pepper boxes on the tables, and ridiculed health reform and its advocates. Is it possible that some Seventh-day Adventist teachers have used their pepper boxes, filled with the most pungent and caustic remarks against educational reforms?

> "It is most difficult to adopt right principles of education after having been long accustomed to popular methods. The first attempt to change old customs brought severe trials upon those who desired to walk in the way which God had pointed out. Mistakes have been made, and great loss has been the result. There have been hindrances which have tended to keep us in common worldly lines, and to prevent us from grasping true educational principles... Some teachers and managers who are only half converted are stumbling blocks to others. They concede some things and make half reforms, but when greater knowledge comes, they refuse to advance, preferring to work according to their own ideas... Reformers have been handicapped, and some have ceased to urge reforms. They seem unable to stem the current of doubt and criticism... We need now to begin over again. Reforms must be entered into with heart and soul and will. Errors may be hoary with age; but age does not make error truth nor truth error." (*Testimonies for the Church*, Vol. 6, pp. 141-142).

The spirit of the reformed:—In the days when the schools of the prophets flourished, the man who had these schools in charge was called "father," and the students were known as "sons." In New Testament times, one of the greatest teachers, barring the Master himself, speaks lovingly of "Timothy, mine own son in the faith;" and "Titus, mine own son after the common faith;" and "My little children of whom I travail in birth." He emphasizes still further the difference between the real teacher and the hired instructor, saying, "For though you have ten thousand instructors in Christ Jesus, I have begotten thee through the gospel." It is this spirit of fatherhood on the part of the teacher that makes for success. Emerson has said, "An institution is the lengthened shadow of one man." That one man is the "father."

We have already seen that many of the failures of the educational reform are to be laid at the feet of timid, unbelieving, conservative teachers; wherever there has been real success, and fruit has been borne in an educational reform movement, you will find one or more teachers who have served as fathers or mothers to the enterprise. As a rule, we must recognize that a school which is obliged to have frequent change of teachers or management, will see few results in the way of steady, healthy, educational reform. Luther and Melanchthon were the parents of Wittenberg, and so long as they remained, the institution was a power for reform throughout Europe.

Jefferson as a father:—When in his 83d year, Jefferson would ride eight or ten miles on horseback over a rough mountain road to the University of Virginia. "This shows the deep interest with which he watched over this child of his old age, and why he preferred the more endearing title of 'father' to that of 'founder.'" Mr. Jefferson carried out this fatherly feeling through the last years of his life, for he used to entertain the students at Sunday dinner in his own home.

> "They might be young and bashful, but he knew the county from which they came, the men with whom they were acquainted, and he gave himself to the student family so completely that they soon felt at home." (*Thomas Jefferson and the University of Virginia*, p. 216).

Oberlin had fathers:—Oberlin could never have accomplished what it did had it lacked this parentage. The relation of the founders to the institution when it was conceived in their minds is expressed in these words as they rose from prayer, "Well, the child is born, and what shall its name be?" (*The Story of Oberlin*, p. 81). Their love for this child was manifested in the same manner that a parent shows love for its offspring; they toiled, sacrificed, and suffered for years without thinking of remuneration. Of Oberlin's faculty it is said,

> "Among them was the conviction which nothing could shake, that the faculty ought to go 'by faith' in the matter of salary; that is, should not insist upon any legal obligation to pay them any definite sum, but be content to receive whatever happened to be forthcoming from the treasury." (*Ibid.*, p. 284).

The spirit of fatherhood on the part of Oberlin men is revealed in the following experience of one worker:

> "[He] was so much delighted with what he found of religious fervor and democratic simplicity, that not long after he cast in his lot with the colonists, bringing several thousand dollars taken from his own purse or gained by solicitation from his friends. Elected a trustee, he was abundant in financial labors." (*Idem*).

The spirit of fatherhood means not only to sacrifice on salary, but to utilize your money and to solicit help from friends.

Mr. Finney also bore this same relationship to the institution. Many tried to entice him to what they liked to call more important fields and better remuneration, but he remained as president of the school for over forty years. As Elijah called Elisha from the plow to a subordinate place in the school of the prophets, that he might be trained to become a father when Elijah should depart, so Finney called Fairchild, a young man who had worked his way through Oberlin. Fairchild was afterwards offered lucrative and popular positions, but he chose to remain with Oberlin as a subordinate to Doctor Finney at four dollars per week, and there received the training which put him at the head of the school when Finney was called away. Fairchild's connection with the school lasted over sixty years.

These men each had a vision. Their students had visions. The fathers and mothers of Oberlin loved their children, and their example was not lost upon the students; for they went everywhere with the same spirit to father some enterprise for the salvation of souls. They never hesitated because a field was considered hard. They were as loyal to a hard field as their teachers before them had been loyal to Oberlin. It led Oberlin students to say, *"Henceforth that land is my country that most needs my help."*

Walking with God, but not with a perfect heart:—Of certain kings of Judah it is written that they "did that which was right in the sight of the Lord but not with a perfect heart." God used Professor Finney and gave him a view of the spiritual condition of the popular churches. He knew what the results would be if they did not reform.

> "Professor Finney of Oberlin College said, 'The churches generally are becoming sadly degenerate. They have gone very far from

the Lord, and He has withdrawn himself from them.'" (*The Great Controversy*, p. 377).

Stewart, Shipherd, President Mahan, all founders of Oberlin, understood the situation as well as Professor Finney. They all recognized that the only sensible way to bring about a permanent reformation in the Protestant denominations was through a system of Christian education, for "the hope of the future missionary work lies with the young." These men fought a good fight. They were all reformers of the highest type. They belong in the class with William Miller, Fitch, Himes, and others.

Oberlin hears the first angel's message as preached by William Miller and Charles Fitch:—

> "William Miller, having long since discovered things most marvelous in Daniel and the Revelation, proceeded for half a generation to turn the world upside down in preparation for the end of this dispensation, which this farmer-prophet fixed for 1943." (*The Story of Oberlin*, p. 66).

> "The Rev. Charles Fitch came to preach the doctrine of the immediate second coming of Christ. He was a man of much personal magnetism, intensely in earnest, profoundly convinced of the truth of his message, and called, as he felt, to bring the better light to the good people of Oberlin." (*Oberlin: The Colony and the College*, p. 86).

The founders were greatly stirred, as were many of the students. But we have already seen the weakness on the part of some Oberlin teachers toward preliminary reforms. We have seen the terribly bitter spirit manifested by most of the denominational leaders. These things almost crushed Oberlin's reforms until she was unable to meet the higher demands made upon her by the midnight cry. Oberlin College was not perfect in her heart, but God rewarded the institution for the loyalty she had shown, and she became a powerful factor in certain reforms in the world's history, although she failed to have a part in that reform of all reforms, the third angel's message. It is well for Seventh-day Adventists to remember that these things happened to Oberlin as an example for those upon whom the ends of the world are come. Oberlin teachers did not "break every yoke" of worldly education, but "placed on the necks of their students worldly yokes instead of the yoke of Christ." To us it is said, "The plan of the schools we shall established in these closing years of the work is to be of an entirely different order than those we have instituted," but Oberlin decided to follow the methods adopted In the older established schools. She yielded to pressure, and thus began that "clinging to old customs, and because of this, we are far behind, where we should be in the development" of God's work. Oberlin men, just before their test came, failed to comprehend the purpose of God in the plans laid before them for the education of their workers. "They adopted methods which retarded the work of God. Years have passed into eternity with small results that might have shown the accomplishment of a great work." Oberlin, by yielding to opposition, unfitted herself to carry the message of present truth in all its fullness to other countries "because she failed to break every educational yoke." She failed at the last to come "into the line of true education," and as a result she could not give the final message to the world.

3. Some Educational Experiences of Seventh-day Adventists

The condition of the Protestant denominations in 1844 is illustrated by the five foolish virgin. When the midnight cry was given in the spring of that year, most of the leaders of these denominations took their stand against it. During the days of preparation, they had failed "to understand the true science of education," and they were not ready when the climax came. Some of their own educational reformers had endeavored to prepare the denominations for this great event, but these educational men were opposed and repulsed by their church leaders. Therefore, the leaders of the church were not ready to accept the first, angel's message. Had the Protestant denominations "come into the line of true education," they would have accepted the first angel's message. This would have United them into one body again.

> "The church would again have reached that blessed state of unity, faith and love which existed in apostolic days when the believers were of one heart and one soul." (*The Great Controversy*, p. 379).

The popular denominations had been called by the Lord to prepare the world for Christ's second coming. They refused to obey, and "about fifty thousand withdrew from the churches." (*Ibid.*, p. 376). From this number came a few stalwart, daring, faithful Christians who became the founders and leaders of the Seventh-day Adventist denomination. The most of these sturdy leaders "had little of the learning of the schools." They had received their education "in the school of Christ, and their humility and obedience make them great." (*Ibid.*, p. 456). They were self-made, and had no need to spend much time to unlearn the wisdom received from that system of education which caused the ruin of the Protestant denominations of 1844.

Elder James White, in his life of William Miller, expresses in the following words his estimate of that system of education which ruined the Protestants:

> "What now would have been the effect of what is called a regular course of education? ... Would it have performed its appropriate work, that of discipling, enlarging, and furnishing the mind, leaving unimpaired by the process its natural energies, self-dependence as to man, and its sense of dependence and accountability as to God? Or, would it have placed him in the crowded ranks of those who are content to share in the honor of repeating the twaddle, true or false, which passes for truth in the school or sect which has made them what they are?" (*Sketches of the Christian Life and Public Labors of William Miller*, pp. 15, 16).

Seventh-day Adventists called to be reformers:—These brave Christian reformers were now facing a situation similar to that faced by the Christian refugees who fled from Europe to the shores of America for the sake of developing a new order of things. But "the English reformers, while denouncing the doctrines of Romanism, had retained many of its forms." (*The Great Controversy*, p. 289). The founders of the Seventh-day Adventist church had left apostate churches, and they, like the English reformers, were impressed with the condition of these churches, but, while denouncing the Papal doctrines found in the apostate Protestant churches, they failed to see all the errors in those churches. The reformers of 1844 also met persecution, as did the English reformers before they came to this country. For of them it is said, "Many were persecuted by their unbelieving brethren." (*Ibid.*, p. 172).

During the first few years of Seventh-day Adventist church history, we find the founders searching the Bible for the great fundamental doctrines of the third angel's message, which revealed false doctrines and certain fallacies that had crept into the popular churches; in writing and publishing those doctrines to the world; and in developing a church organization. They did their work well.

But what was being done for the education of the children and youth during this constructive period? Many of them were attending those same schools that had heretofore trained men to repudiate the light of the first angel's message. Many of the reformers were disturbed over the situation. They began to realize that keeping the children in these school would, in time, lead these children to regard truth as did their teachers who were out of sympathy with the message.

Light came from God on the problem of education. Seventh-day Adventist parents were instructed to take their children out of the public schools, and to establish schools offering a Christian training.

> "When I was shown by the angel of God that an institution should be established for the education of our youth, I saw that it would be one of the greatest means ordained of God for the salvation of souls." (*Christian Education*, p. 25).

To establish schools seemed too great a task to the majority of our people at that time. It was like the conquest of Canaan to the children of Israel. Many children from Adventist homes were taken out of the worldly schools, but the church lacked faith to establish schools and to grasp the Lord's promise to provide Christian teachers. So, for a time, the children were left without any school advantages. Parents realized that something must be done, but as they had not faith to obey the word of God in this matter, they gradually returned the young people to the worldly schools. Thus began the wanderings of Seventh-day Adventists in the wilderness of worldly education. They failed to understand "the true science of education." The work was retarded, and "because of this we are far behind where we should be in the development of the third angel's message." This experience came about the year 1860; in the year 1901, forty Years after, this word came, "It is the beginning of the educational reform."

The following instruction came during this wandering in the educational wilderness:

> "There should have been in past generations provisions made for education upon a larger scale. In connection with the schools should have been agricultural and manufacturing establishments. There should have been teachers also of household labor. There should have been a portion of the time each day devoted to labor, that the physical and mental might be equally exercised. If schools had been established upon the plan we have mentioned, there would not now be so many unbalanced minds... Had the system of education generations back been conducted upon altogether a different plan, the youth of

this generation would not now be so depraved and worthless." (*Christian Education*, pp. 18, 11).

From the pages of the *Review and Herald* we gather that there was considerable agitation over educational matters until the founding of Battle Creek College in 1874. By this time many of the leaders began to understand more fully the results of the terrible mistake made by not following the instruction given in the fifties concerning education. The need of schools was apparent. Brother A. Smith, writing for the *Review and Herald* (Vol. 40, No. 2) said,

> "Any one at all acquainted with our common schools is aware that the influences of their associations is terrible upon the morals of our children... I do not know why young ladies could not qualify themselves by a course of study at Battle Creek to serve as teachers of select schools in our large churches."

This contains a suggestion for church schools.

A church school was established in Battle Creek about this time. The teacher, who was the prime mover in this enterprise, was an educational reformer, and if the reform that he advocated had been favorably received and intelligently practiced, Seventh-day Adventists would have come out of the educational wilderness long before they did. The ideas on education which this man held were similar to the reforms taught prior to 1844. God desired that when educational work did begin among Seventh-day Adventists it should be on a basis at least equal to the educational reform movement before 1844. God had sent Seventh-day Adventists an educator who had accepted the third angel's message, and who was ready to begin the educational work among us at the point where the educational reforms ceased before 1944. This reform work accepted, would have placed Seventh-day Adventist educational work in a position before the world corresponding to that held by Seventh-day Adventist sanitarium work. The first Seventh-day Adventist sanitarium came quickly into line with all of the advanced ideas taught and practiced before 1844. And if there is one thing above another that has distinguished Seventh-day Adventists before the world, it has been their health reform principles and sanitarium work. They had an equal chance in the educational world.

The following words show what a serious mistake was made when this educational reformer who had come among us was criticized and his reforms rejected:

> "The present age is one of show and surface work in education. Brother _____ possesses naturally a love for system and thoroughness, and these have become habit by lifelong training and discipline. He has been approved of God for this. His labors are of real worth because he will not allow students to be superficial. But in his very first efforts toward the establishment of a school he encountered many obstacles... Some of the parents neglected to sustain the school, and their children did not respect the teacher because he wore poor clothing... The Lord approved of the general course of Brother _____, as he was laying the foundation for the school which is now in operation." (*Testimony for the Church*, Vol. 5, pp. 90, 91).

This church school developed into Battle Creek College.

Battle Creek College should have been established on the land:— The promoters of Battle Creek College were instructed to establish the school on a large tract of land where various industries might be carried on and the school made a manual training institution, and conducted according to educational reform ideas. The following statement, which appears in the *General Conference Bulletin*, 1901, page 217, was made by Elder Haskell regarding the founding of Battle Creek College:

> "I remember the time when the present site was selected for the location of the College here in Battle Creek... Sister White, in talking to the locating committee, said, 'Get the school on some land outside of the thickly-settled city, where the students can work on the land.'"

In the same *General Conference Bulletin*, pages 115 and 116, is the following statement from Mrs. E. G. White concerning the location of Battle Creek College:

> "Some may be stirred by the transfer of the school from Battle Creek, but they need not be. This move is in accordance with God's design for the school before the institution was established, but men could not see how this could be done. There were so many who said the school must be in Battle Creek. Now we say that it must be somewhere else. The best thing that can be done is to dispose of the school's buildings here as soon as possible. Begin at once to look for a place where the school can be conducted on right lines... Get an extensive tract of land, and here begin the work which I entreated should be

> commenced before the school was established here... Our schools should be located away from the cities on a large tract of land so the students will have opportunity to do manual work."

From the above we see that when Battle Creek College was established there was not enough faith and courage to build up an educational institution among Adventists in the country on a farm as the educational reformers prior to 1844 located their schools. The cause of this inability to appreciate the system of education for which God was calling was due to the fact, that the leading men of the denomination had received their education in schools that had repudiated the reform ideas advocated before 1844. The importance of manual training and kindred reforms had not been impressed upon their minds as Oberlin during her reform experience had stamped those ideas into the minds of her students. Then, too, Seventh-day Adventists, a number of years before the establishment of their first college, lacked the faith to obey God in establishing simple schools on the right plan for educating the children that should have been taken out of the public schools. Those Adventist children whose parents, for lack of faith, failed to take them from the public schools, were now among the leaders of the denomination. Their faith and courage in the educational reform were weak, and their eyes were as blind to the true science of Christian education as were the eyes of their parents who had failed to provide Christian schools for them. The idea is thus expressed,

> "If ministers and teachers could have a full sense of their responsibility, we should see a different state of things in the world today, but they are too narrow in their views and purposes. They do not realize the importance of their work or its results." (*Christian Education*, p. 24).

And so, because of unbelief, the first college was established where God said it should not be, and in the place of the reform principles and methods of Christian education, there were introduced the principles, methods, ways, studies, and ideals of the colleges of the Protestant denominations round about them. Therefore, under these circumstances, in this institution, were to be trained the future missionaries for the denomination—those missionaries who should avoid the mistakes in preparing for the loud cry that ensnared the young people of the Protestant denominations before 1844 when approaching the midnight cry.

Results of the failure:—Our first college soon began to bear an abundant crop of worldly educational fruit, and the Lord gives plainly his estimate of this fruit and the system that produced it, and some sound advice as to the best course to pursue.

> "If a worldly influence is to bear sway in our school, then sell it out to worldlings and let them take the entire control; and those who have invested their means in that institution will establish another school, to be conducted, not upon the plan of popular schools, nor according to the desires of principal and teachers, but upon the plan which God has specified... Our college stands today in a position that God does not approve." (*Testimonies for the Church*, Vol. 5, pp. 25, 27).

A chance for reform:—It is not our purpose to enter into the history of Battle Creek College. It did much good, but its location and the system first adopted made it difficult to carry out Christian educational reform. However, at different times, strong efforts were made to bring about reforms. The following statement tells concisely the entire history of Battle Creek College:

> "Our institutions of learning may swing into worldly conformity. Step by step they may advance to the world; but they are prisoners of hope, and God will correct and enlighten them, and bring them back to their upright position of distinction from the world." (*Fundamentals of Christian Education*, p. 290 [Jan. 9, 1894]).

Battle Creek College in Battle Creek, like Israel of old, swung back and forth between God's plan and the world's system of education. But she was a "prisoner of hope," and, as already stated by Mrs. White in the *General Conference Bulletin* of 1901, God brought her back to her upright position. In other words, He put her on the land where He said she should be founded, and where she could carry out the principles of Christian education.

We have seen that God sent clear and positive instruction to guide Seventh-day Adventist leaders in the location and establishment of their first college. We have been told that this instruction was not wholly carried out. Their faith was not strong enough for them to attempt to carry out this and other most important and fundamental principles of Christian education, such principles as making the Bible the basis of all the subjects taught; the discarding of harmful literature; the eliminating of traditional courses and their degrees; the making of physiology the basis of every educational effort; manual training; agricultural work; reform in buildings, diet, etc.

Seventh-day Adventists cling to Papal education:—Their failure in all these directions was due to the same experience that caused the English reformers to fail in laying a foundation for educational work that would have qualified an army of Christian missionaries to give the first angel's message. "The English reformers, while renouncing the doctrines of Romanism, had retained many of its forms." (*The Great Controversy*, p. 289). We have learned that while the English reformers broke away from Papal doctrines to a large extent through ignorance of the results they did not hesitate to adopt bodily the Papal system of education. They thought that sandwiching in a little Bible, and flavoring their teaching with some religious instruction, constituted Christian education. They were mistaken. The long history of spiritual failures in this country was the fruit. As a result of this ignorance, the Protestant churches were led down to a condition where they very closely resembled the Papacy itself and were called Babylon. Our own Seventh-day Adventist leaders left these Protestant denominations as the English reformers left the European Papal churches. They broke away from the Papal doctrines held by the Protestant churches, just as did the English reformers. But, like those English reformers, they carried with them, from the Protestant denominations, an educational system that was Papal in spirit. The English reformers struggled for years to stem the current of apostasy. They failed to understand the philosophy of their declining religious experience. Nevertheless, the results came at last, dreadful but sure; they were morally ruined and cast aside because they had failed "to come into the line of true education." It was a beautiful prospect utterly destroyed by the wiles of the arch deceiver. It was made possible through ignorance of the principles of Christian education on the part of many great and good men.

In these last days Satan will, if possible, deceive the very elect. Is there any reason why he should not use the same method which has proved so effectual in his hands through all the ages—in the overthrow of the Jewish church and the apostolic church; in neutralizing, through the Jesuits, the great sixteenth century Reformation; in thwarting the efforts of the English reformers who attempted to establish on the shores of America the church for its final struggle?

Let us again trace the present system of worldly education to its source. The educational plan of our first college was borrowed largely from the popular religious colleges of the Protestant denominations. These denominations received their educational light from the older educational institutions of this country such as Harvard and Yale; Harvard and Yale, as we have seen, borrowed theirs from Oxford and Cambridge; Oxford and Cambridge are daughters of Paris University; Paris University, presided over by the papists, was wholly Papal, and is the mother of European Universities; she borrowed her educational system from Pagan Rome; Pagan Rome 'gathered into its arms the elements of Grecian and oriental culture;" Grecian schools drew their wisdom and inspiration from Egypt.

> "The ancients looked upon Egypt as a school of wisdom. Greece sent thither her illustrious philosophers and lawgivers-Pythagoras and Plato, Lycurgus and Solon—to complete their studies... Hence even the Greeks in ancient times were accustomed to borrow their politics and their learning from the Egyptians. (*A History of Education*, p. 32-34).

Egypt, therefore, must be recognized as the source of all worldly wisdom that is worth studying. This worldly system of education from Egypt is certainly enduring, or it would not have come down to us through these long ages. It is this very Egyptian spirit of philosophy that has made so called classical literature so attractive to men of this world. The wisdom of Egypt has been kept alive in the world by students, who, while in school, have studied her philosophy and have caught their inspiration from the classics. Strange to say, the most potent factor in keeping this Egyptian education alive has been the Christian church itself. For various reasons, at different times, she has not only allowed but encouraged her young people to study these writings. Again and again the church has been deceived by this Egyptian wisdom as Eve was deceived by the knowledge of good and evil. Christians have clothed this subtle philosophy with a Christian garb (Do you recognize the Papacy?) and scattered it broadcast.

This egyptian philosophy ruined every church up to 1844, and Seventh-day Adventists have been told that "now as never before we need to understand the true science of education. If we fail to understand this we shall never have a place in the kingdom of God." It is against this Egyptian philosophy that God warns us in the words just quoted. It is this very philosophy, so subtle, that God has in mind when He warns the church that "If possible 'he' (Satan) shall deceive the very elect." We young Seventh-day Adventists should study the man Moses, who, "learned in all the wisdom of the Egyptians," a graduate from the highest educational institution of the world, and recognized as an intellectual giant, forsook all the things that Egyptian education made it possible for him to enjoy, and entered God's training school in the wilderness.

> "It was not the teachings of the schools of Egypt that enabled Moses to triumph over all his enemies, but an ever-abiding faith, an unflinching faith, a faith that did not fail under the most trying circumstances." (*Fundamentals of Christian Education*, pp. 345-346).

After spending forty years in forgetting his worldly education and obtaining the wisdom of God, Moses was qualified to stand at the head of the largest industrial school ever known. "What an industrial school was that in the wilderness!" (*Education*, p. 37). It took the students in this school another forty years to break the yoke of Egypt's educational system and to understand "the true science of education" so that they might have a place in the land of Canaan.

Christ calls men away from the Egyptian system of education:— But the most important thing for us Seventh-day Adventist young people is to study the great Teacher of whom it is said, "Out of Egypt have I called my Son." So completely was the Son of God called out of Egypt that as a child He was never permitted to attend even the Jewish church schools because they were so saturated with Egyptian worldly education. Seventh-day Adventist children have an equal chance. Study the Master in the humble home school at Nazareth, in the, shop and on the farm, on the hills and in the valleys. He grew in wisdom until, at the age of twelve, he astonished the leaders of the church with the fruit of Christian education.

> "Mark the features of Christ's work... Although His followers were fishermen, He did not advise them to go first into the school of the rabbis before entering upon the work" (*Fundamentals of Christian Education*, p. 359).

Why? Because the schools of the Rabbis were filled with Greek and Egyptian philosophy which blinds the eyes to spiritual truth. It was to a teacher from one of these schools that Christ said, "Ye must be born again."

God pleads with us to establish schools for our children that they may obtain His wisdom and understanding even in their tender years. Seventh-day Adventist students should forever turn their backs on this system of worldly education—the wisdom of Egypt—that has wrecked the prospects of every Christian church up to the Seventh-day Adventist. And we, individually, are in danger of this same Egyptian wisdom.

> "I am filled with sadness when I think of our condition as a people. The Lord has not closed heaven to us, but our own course of continual backsliding has separated us from God... And yet the general opinion is that the church is flourishing and that peace and spiritual prosperity are in all her borders. The church has turned back from following Christ her Leader and is steadily retreating toward Egypt." (*Testimonies for the Church*, p. 217).

Before 1844 the Spirit of God sent messages to the Protestant denominations telling them of their condition in language very similar to that just quoted. They failed to understand it, because, as we have seen, the Papal system of education, which they unwittingly introduced into their church schools, had put out their spiritual eyesight, and had deafened their ears to the word of God. They did not understand "the true science of education;" they did not "come into the line of true education;" and they were rejected. The student of educational history knows the force of the statement, "The church is steadily retreating toward Egypt," for this Papal system of education has its roots in Egyptian learning and philosophy, away from which God forever called His ancient people. Realizing the results that have come to other Christian bodies, we might be discouraged as we see our first school patterned largely after the colleges of the popular churches, especially in view of the fact that

> "the customs and practices of the Battle Creek school go forth to all the churches, and the pulse heartbeats of that school are felt throughout the body of believers." (*Fundamentals of Christian Education*, p. 223).

But we have the good promise of our God,

> "Our institutions of learning may swing into worldly conformity. Step by step they may advance to the world; but they are prisoners of

hope, and God will correct and enlighten them, and bring them back to their upright position of distinction from the world. I am watching with intense interest, hoping to see our schools thoroughly imbued with the spirit of true and undefiled religion. When the students are thus imbued, they will see that there is a great work to be done in the lines in which Christ worked, and the time they have given to amusements will be given up to doing earnest missionary work." (*Ibid.*, p. 290 [Jan. 9, 1894]).

Seventh-day Adventists called to be reformers:—Every loyal Seventh-day Adventist, realizing the parentage of our educational institutions, and the hope extended to them, will endeavor to help bring to an upright position every school found out of harmony with the divine plan. Every method used in our schools should be subjected to the divine test. "To the law, and to the testimony; if they speak not according to this word it is because there is no light in them." Everything should be discarded that does not prove to be genuine. Instead of treating the situation lightly or indulging in reactionary criticism, as men have treated reforms of the past, especially those reforms of 1834-1844, let us study prayerfully the following instruction:

"We need now to begin over again. Reforms must be entered into with heart and soul and will. Errors may be hoary with age, but age does not make truth error nor error truth. Altogether too long have the old customs and habits been followed. The Lord would now have every idea that is false put away from teachers and students... That which the Lord has spoken concerning the instruction to be given in our schools is to be strictly regarded; for if there is not in some respects an education of an altogether different character from that which has been carried on in some of our schools, we need not have gone to the expense of purchasing land and erecting school buildings." (*Testimonies for the Church*, Vol. 6, p. 142).

Battle Creek College the model for other schools:—As Battle Creek College was the first school among us, her example was followed by practically every other school established by the denomination. They modeled their schools after her course of study; they imitated her methods of teaching; and to a large extent followed her plan of location and patterned their buildings after hers.

"The customs and practices of the Battle Creek school go forth to all the churches, and the pulse heartbeats of that school are felt throughout the body of believers." (*Fundamentals of Christian Education*, p. 224).

These facts should help us to better understand the statement made when it was decided to move Battle Creek College out of Battle Creek on to a farm.

"We are thankful that an interest is being shown in the work of establishing schools on a right foundation, as they should have been established years ago." (*General Conference Bulletin*, 1901, p. 455).

The second school established among Adventists was located at Healdsburg, California. An attempt was made by the promoters of this school to follow the Lord's instruction in the matter of location. While Healdsburg was not located in the city as was Battle Creek College, yet, like Lot, the founders begged to go into a little city. Healdsburg College was located on the edge of a small town. While they endeavored to establish the manual labor feature, their unfortunate location on a small piece of ground, the retaining of traditional courses and degrees, and the strong influence exerted by Battle Creek College, soon swung Healdsburg into worldly conformity. But the words of hope were spoken to her also:

"Step by step they may advance to the world; but they are prisoners of hope, and God will correct and enlighten them, and bring them back to their upright position of distinction from the world." (*Fundamentals of Christian Education*, p. 290).

Over a quarter of a century after her establishment, Healdsburg College was moved to a large tract of land near St. Helena, California, and the college in its new location was in a position to begin its educational reform, as Battle Creek College is said to have come to its upright position when reestablished on the land.

In Volume 6 of the *Testimonies*, page 139, our people are told,

"Schools should be established, not such elaborate schools as those at Battle Creek and College View, but more simple schools with more humble buildings and with teachers who will adopt the same plans that were followed in the schools of the prophets."

Again, in the same volume we are told, "We need now to begin over again. Reforms must be entered into with heart and soul and will." (*Ibid.*, p. 142). We have seen the necessity for Battle Creek College and Healdsburg College to begin their work over again. The teachers in these schools now have a chance to "adopt the same plans which were followed in the schools of the prophets," and to enter the educational reforms "with heart and soul and will."

Traditional courses:—One of the leading reforms called for in the Papal system of education deals with the question of courses and their degrees, because the moral fall of the Protestant churches can be attributed almost directly to the traditional courses offered in their schools and the attendant degrees. As a rule, their ministers were obliged to finish a course and obtain a degree, and this often affected their independence in following God's word; it checked their individuality and their originality. The school men are said to be

> "a stereotype representation of what the course makes them; if they (the graduates) raise a fellowman out of the mire, they never get him nearer to heaven than the school where they were educated... They are content to share in the honor of repeating the twaddle, true or false, which passes for truth, in the school or sect which has made them what they are." (*Sketches of the Christian Life and Public Labors of William Miller*, p. 16).

The primitive christians carried the gospel rapidly and effectively to the world. In their school they taught only those subjects that would prepare the student to do the Lord's work. By the world their educators were regarded as "odd, singular, straight-laced extremists." Everything was done by these Christian educators to prepare the student quickly to act the part of a good soldier in the battle. Students were not detained in the school to finish a course or take a degree, a custom in vogue in the worldly schools. Later, half converted pagan-Christian teachers introduced the course-and-degree idea which developed an educational trust controlled by the church leaders, and no one was allowed to teach or preach until he had finished a course and received a degree.

One of the most serious objections brought against this plan is that it closes the mind of the student to truth. Practically every religious reform has come through humble laymen because the church leaders, as a rule, in obtaining their education, have become conservative. Conservatism is the result of passing, through a rigid, mechanical course of study for a degree.

The student is held in a rut, on a treadmill; he is described as ever going and never getting anywhere. Consequently when the truth is presented to these school men, especially if it is brought by a layman, it is not looked upon with favor, as they have come to regard themselves as the regular channel through which light must come to the people. The truth of this statement is borne out by historical facts. Motley, giving the experience of reformers in Holland, writes thus of the restriction placed on laymen by the Papal system of education:

> "We forbid all lay persons *to converse or dispute concerning* the Holy Scriptures, openly or secretly, especially on any doubtful or difficult matters, or *to read, teach,* or *expound* the *Scriptures*, unless they have duly studied theology and have been approved by some renowned university." (John Lothrop Motley, *The Rise of the Dutch Republic*, p. 134 [In One Volume, Ed. of 1863]).

He adds, however, that

> "to the ineffable disgust of the conservatives in church and state here were men with little education, utterly devoid of Hebrew, of lowly station—hatters, curriers, tanners, dyers and the likes—who began to preach; remembering unreasonably, perhaps, that the early disciples selected by the Founder of Christianity had not all been Doctors of Theology with diplomas from renowned universities." (*Ibid.*, p. 264).

The Lord sees that the rigid course with the degree often brings into the church "many men after the flesh... many mighty ... many noble," instead of making leaders who realize that "God hath chosen the foolish things of the world to confound the wise ... that no flesh should glory in his presence."

The most of the school men about 1844 rejected the first angel's message because it did not come to them in the regular way. "The fact that the message was, to a great extent, preached by laymen, was urged as an argument against it. ... Multitudes, trusting implicitly in their pastors, refused to listen to the warning." (*The Great Controversy*, p. 380).

Seventh-day Adventists will be tried on this same point:—"As the time comes for it [the third angel's message] to be given with great-est power, the Lord will work through humble instruments, leading the minds of those who consecrate themselves to His service. The laborers will be qualified rather by the unction of His Spirit than by the training of literary institutions." (*The Great Controversy*, p. 606).

Satan will work with all his power of deception to have a company of men at the head of the Seventh-day Adventist church at the time of the loud cry who will regard the work of humble instruments led by the Spirit of God, who have not graduated from a literary institution, with the same disfavor as the leaders of the Protestant churches before 1844 regarded such irregularities. God wants thousands of men trained in our schools, but He does not want them to receive such a training that their attitude toward truth will be the same as that of the school men of other denominations prior to 1844. The question of most vital importance to us Seventh-day Adventists is, can we obtain a liberal, practical education for God's work without being spoiled in the training? There must be some way out.

When Battle Creek College was encouraging students to take courses leading to degrees modeled after the worldly schools, it received the following instruction: "The students themselves would not think of such a delay in entering the work if it were not urged upon them by those who are supposed to be shepherds and guardians." This system was described as, "This long drawn out process, adding and adding more time, more branches." The Lord expressed His disfavor in these words,

> "The preparation of the students has been managed on the same principle as have the building operations... God is calling, and has been calling for years, for a reform on these lines... While so much is spent to put a few through an exhaustive course of study, there are many who are thirsting for the knowledge they could get in a few months; one or two years would be considered a great blessing. Give students a start, but do not feel that it is your duty to carry them year after year. It is their duty to get out into the field to work." (*Fundamentals of Christian Education*, pp. 337, 338).

> "The student should not permit himself to be bound down to any particular course of studies involving long periods of time, but should be guided in such matters by the Spirit of God... I would warn the students not to advance one step in these lines,—not even upon the advice of their instructors or men in positions of authority,—unless they have first sought God individually, with their hearts thrown open to the influence of the Holy Spirit, and obtained His counsel concerning the contemplated course of study. Let every selfish desire

to distinguish yourselves be set aside... With many students the motive and aim which caused them to enter school have gradually been lost sight of, and an unholy ambition to secure a high class education has led them to sacrifice the truth... There are many who are crowding too many studies into a limited period of time... I would advise restriction in following those methods of education which imperil the soul and defeat the purpose for which time and money are spent. Education is a grand life work... After a period of time has been devoted to study, let no one advise students to enter again upon a line of study, but rather advise them to enter upon the work for which they have been studying. Let them be advised to put into practice the theories they have gained... Those who are directing the work of education are placing too large an amount of study before those who have come to Battle Creek to fit up for the work of the Master. They have supposed it was necessary for them to go deeper and deeper into educational lines; and while they are pursuing various courses of study, year after year of precious time is passing away." (*Ibid.*, pp. 347-353).

"The thought to be kept before students is that time is short, and that they must make speedy preparation for doing the work that is essential for this time... Understand that I say nothing in these words to depreciate education, but to warn those who are in danger of carrying that which is lawful to unlawful extremes." (*Ibid.*, pp. 354, 357).

The results of following this plan of education is well illustrated by the experiences of Battle Creek College when it was working hard to follow the traditional courses leading to degrees which her faculty hoped would be looked upon with favor by the world. The following words show the danger from receiving such an education:

"The Holy Spirit has often come to our schools and has not been recognized, but has been treated as a stranger, perhaps even as an intruder." "Again and again the heavenly messenger has been sent to the school." "The Great Teacher Himself was among you. How did you honor Him? Was He a stranger to some of the educators?" (*Counsels to Parents, Teachers and Students*, pp. 68, 370, 363).

It is with shame and sadness that we are compelled to acknowledge that we teachers were as dead, spiritually, to the heavenly Teacher as were school men to the first angel before 1844. The greatest objection raised against the Holy Spirit instructing teachers as to the right ways of conducting the school at the time was that it would take students from their regular studies and disturb their plans for finishing a course and receiving degrees. Much instruction was sent to the school on the subject of long and rigid courses, but the teachers and students of Battle Creek College, to a large extent, turned away from the instruction of the heavenly visitant. We must remember that Battle Creek College had not been established in the place that the Spirit directed. It did not follow the pattern for its establishment; it did not even attempt to introduce and practice the important educational reforms revealed by the Lord before 1844, but was content to get its ideas, life and inspiration from the colleges of those religious denominations that had rejected the first angel's message.

We have already read that "the customs and practices of the Battle Creek School go forth to all the churches, and the pulse heart beats of that school are felt throughout the body of believers." We must, therefore, conclude that as all the churches and believers were more or less under the influence of Battle Creek College at this time, at least a large per cent of Seventh-day Adventists would have treated the heavenly visitant, had He come to them suggesting reforms, as the Battle Creek College teachers and students treated Him. Perhaps, then, we can understand why God says,

> "The plan of the schools we shall establish in these closing years of the work is to be of an entirely different order from those we have established… I have been shown that in our educational work we are not to follow the methods that have been adopted in our older established schools. There is among us too much clinging to old customs, and because of this we are far behind where we should be in the development of the third angel's message." ("The Madison School," p. 29).

The founders of Battle Creek College made their mistake when they did not follow the plan given them by the Lord, but modeled the school after worldly schools about them. In these last days your test will come. You are not to pattern your schools after the older established Seventh-day Adventist schools, but are to follow the divine model. If we fail to understand this divine plan, we shall have no place in the loud cry.

Reform called for:—The teachers of Battle Creek College at that time received this word:

> "A succession of showers from the Living Waters has come to you at Battle Creek… Each shower was a consecrated inflowing of divine influence; but you did not recognize it as such. instead of drinking copiously of the streams of salvation so freely offered through the

influence of the Holy Spirit, you turned to common sewers, and tried to satisfy your soul thirst with the polluted waters of human science. The result has been parched hearts in the school and in the church... But I hope the teachers have not yet passed the line where they are given over to hardness of heart and blindness of mind. If they are again visited by the Holy Spirit I hope they will not call righteousness sin and sin righteousness. There is need of heart conversions among the teachers. A genuine change of thoughts and methods of teaching is required to place them where they will have a personal relation to a living Savior... God will come near to the students because they are misled by the educators in whom they put confidence." (*Fundamentals of Christian Education*, pp. 434, 435).

The instruction which came to Battle Creek College for years shows that during all those years the institution was unsettled on many of the important principles of Christian education. She was born with false ideas of education in her constitution, and she did not realize the source of her weakness. She was drinking from streams polluted more or less with worldly wisdom, but she did not know her danger. She was an educational germ carrier, and failed to realize that also. The straight testimonies sent to the institution must convince any believer in the testimonies that Battle Creek College was in great need of educational reform.

Battle Creek College made radical reforms not long after these words were sent. It dropped the regular degree courses, and at the same time enriched the curriculum with a number of subjects very practical for the Seventh-day Adventist missionary, and "liberty in the choice of studies was regarded as fundamental." (*Education in the United States*, p. 197). Each student, with the aid of the teachers, selected those studies considered most essential to his life work. The strength of the faculty was thrown heavily upon those subjects that had been neglected and for which God had been calling for years. When the school broke away from the stereotype courses and degrees, it found itself much more capable of following the instruction sent by the Lord, and the result was that in a short time Battle Creek College was planted on a beautiful farm. It was given an opportunity to get into an upright position, and then this most remarkable statement came "It is the beginning of the educational reform." "No educational institution can place itself in opposition to the errors and corruptions of this degenerate age without receiving threats and insults, but time will place such an institution upon an elevated platform." (*General Conference Bulletin*, 1901, p. 454).

This subject has been treated so fully because some of you students question why we do not arrange studies in courses leading to degrees. You should know where you stand, and why you stand there, and should ask, "Am I following the plan instituted by Battle Creek College, which effected seriously every church in the denomination, or am I following that other plan of which the Lord said, "It is the beginning of educational reform?"

Degrees and what they lead to:—Degrees have been indirectly referred to, for they are the reward of the traditional courses. Were it not for the degree, it would be impossible to hold most students to a pre-scribed course. However, the most dangerous element in degree granting does not seem to be comprehended by those Christian educators who cling to the custom. A degree is a sign or seal of authority. In the Christian church "the conferring of degrees was originated by a pope" as a sign of his authority over the educational system. Today degrees are conferred by the State, and the State has no right to set its seal to the work of an institution unless it can approve the system of education offered by that school. The degree is a sign of its approval. Any Seventh-day Adventist school that grants degrees, thereby invites State inspection, and must accept the world's standard and come into conformity to the worldly system of education. Claiming to conduct Christian schools, we yet seek to so teach that we can satisfy the worldly system. In time the State will either demand absolute conformity to her system or refuse to grant the degrees. If we are building up our work in such a manner as to encourage students to seek degrees, there is great danger that we will compromise on the true science of education in order to retain the State's seal or mark. Seventh-day Adventists are not ignorant of the fact that even today the Papacy has the control practically of all education, and in a short time this will be openly avowed. Then the inspection of our degree granting schools will be done directly by the Papacy, and a degree, if granted, will again come directly from that organization. It will be a seal or a mark of the beast. Other

Protestants failed here. What shall we Seventh-day Adventist students do? One educator has summed up the whole degree question as follows:

> "From his first introduction into the school, to the taking of his final degree, teachers, parents, and doting friends conspire in their efforts to stimulate the boy to get ahead of some one else. Men wear degrees as women wear fine bonnets, jewels in their hair, rings in their ears and on their fingers, and gay ribbons flaunting in the breeze. Consider, for example, the ornamental value of A.M., M.S., Ph.D., or the social value of such a tremendous decorative combination as that enjoyed by Mr. James Brown, A.M., Ph.D., LL.D., D.D. Each one of these titles costs as much as a diamond of moderate size, or a large pearl (not the Pearl of great price), and is worn for practically the same reason. It does not necessarily indicate anything. John Smith, tailor; James Brown, blacksmith; Mr. Jones, surveyor, are examples of titles which produce in the mind something more than the mere decorative effect. These indicate the trade or profession by which the man gains his livelihood."

Because the degree simply puts the possessor in a position which distinguishes him from those who do not hold one, and is not an indication of power to accomplish, worldly men who are building up an educational Aristocracy feel that it is necessary to protect themselves by limiting the degree conferring power. They say, "There should be legislation regulating the granting of academic degrees." The following extract from a report signed by a number of presidents of leading universities appeared in the columns of the Educational Review,

> "The degree conferring power is not to be granted to any institution having requirements for admission and for graduation lower than the minimum standard established by the commission, or to any institution whose productive endowment is not equal to at least $100,000.00. The law is an admirable one, and ought to be adopted by every state in the union in order that wild cat education may go the way of wild cat banking." (Nicholas Murray Butler, *Educational Review*, 1891, vol. 16, p. 103).

You will be interested in the following statement contained in a letter, written by the Educational Secretary of the Seventh-day Adventist denomination in 1896, concerning an interview with Mrs. E. G. White on this subject:

"I explained to her the significance of the degrees and the meaning which was attached to them, and the general course of study which was implied by them in the eyes of other educators, and her idea seemed to be that there is no need that we should pay attention to these things; that what we want to do is to educate for usefulness here and the eternal kingdom hereafter; and that the question with our people is not whether a young man has a degree, but whether he has a suitable preparation so that he can be a blessing to others in this work... I should want to feel perfectly free to arrange the work just as I thought would be best for the young people and for the work, without being bound by the idea that you must maintain a course of study so that you can consistently grant degrees."

The object of our schools should be to prepare students to carry the message of Christ's second coming to all the world, and to prepare them speedily.

"His work is not to wait while His servants go through such wonderfully elaborate preparations as our schools are planning to give." (*Fundamentals of Christian Education*, p. 346).

Let us hope that Seventh-day Adventists may save themselves from those pitfalls that caught the Protestant denominations before 1844.

4. Educational Principles

"Before we carry the message of present truth in all its fullness to other countries, we must first break every yoke. We must come into the line of true education walking in the wisdom of God, and not in the wisdom of the world. God calls for messengers who will be true reformers. We must educate, educate, to prepare a people who will understand the message, and then give the message to the world." ("The Madison School," p. 30).

The object of these studies has been to aid you students to understand the instruction in the paragraph just read, that you may avoid the educational pitfalls, and that you may "come into the line of true education," and have a part in carrying the message to the world.

We shall review briefly the subject, and list important educational principles found in both systems. As these are presented, determine your attitude to each one, and ascertain your reason for taking that position. You are asked to do this with the hope that it will strengthen your position on educational questions, and aid you to "come into the line of true education," and thus be better prepared to carry the message of Christ's soon coming. It is done with the hope that you may more fully sense the deep significance of the statement,

> "Now as never before we need to understand the true science of education. If we fail to understand this, we shall never have a place in the kingdom of God." (*Christian Educator*, August 1, 1897).

1. Protestants hold their children in the church when they receive Christian education. They lose these children when they attend schools having a Papal system. Melanchthon said, "Religion cannot be maintained without them (schools)."

2. The Papal system of education is never a fit model for Protestant schools. Luther and Melanchthon recognized this. Accordingly they

reformed the school system, changing the curriculum, text books, and methods of teaching.

3. Some schools, Christian in form, follow the Papal system, sandwiching in a little Bible, and flavoring the course with Protestant theology. John Sturm did this. So have some schools since the days of Sturm.

4. This combination educational system—Christian and Papal mixed—always opens the way for hairsplitting theological controversies, and the students are neglected for heresy hunting. It always terminates in a victory for Papacy over Protestantism.

5. The Papal system of education makes a Moloch of abstract subjects and worships at his shrine. Its strength lies in repeating meaningless forms, and "a dead study of words takes the place of a living knowledge of things." Mental cramming and formal memorizing are exalted methods of its teachers. Emulation, prizes and rewards are needed stimulants for "a mechanical and compulsory drill in unintelligible formulas," and their long stereotype courses end in degrees, the sign or mark of the system. It is the subjugation of human minds to the authority of some one above, the stifling of free thought by unnatural, close supervision in place of self-government. It leads away from nature, nature's work and nature's God, and centralizes in cities and man-made institutions. This is Papal education, and its reward is the degree conferred at the end of the traditional course.

6. Every school is the pulse beat of some organization;—of the State, if it is a state school; of the Papacy, if a Papal school; and of the Christian church if it is a Christian school. Any educational system which mechanically teaches a stereotype course leading to degrees, will, in time, result in the development of a creed by its controlling organization—a creed written, or perhaps consisting only of the opinions of those in power, but a creed nevertheless, according to which every one not recognizing its power to initiate is considered irregular or independent.

7. Protestant education allows the student freedom in the choice of studies. This freedom from the stereotype course bears fruit in a church which provides for differences of opinion without the cry of heresy. Courses and degrees are an essential element in a religious trust. Trusts,

in the very nature of things, can make no use of those who question their authority; those who differ must be crushed.

8. There are but two systems of education, one inspired by the Word of God and one by other literature. The Christian school not only has Bible study in its curriculum, but Bible principles are the guide of the student's life, and the spirit of the Bible is the inspiration of the school. If Bible principles are not the foundation of all subjects and the basis of all teaching, that school, even though Christian in name, has imbibed Papal principles. Oberlin, breaking from the Papal system before 1844, "restored the Bible to its place as a permanent text book," and pagan and infidel authors were thrown out.

9. Any system of education that exalts the Bible will receive light on health reform, simplicity of dress, country life, etc. Oberlin, preparing for the midnight cry before 1844, accepted light on these subjects. Students discarded the use of flesh foods, tobacco, condiments, tea and coffee, rich pastries, hot breads, they used graham flour, discarded sloppy foods, expensive dress, jewelry, accepted the country as God's home for man, etc. These same reforms will be carried to completion by those who are preparing for the loud cry.

10. Christian schools are content with simple, modest buildings and equipment, but must give great and mighty truth. Papal schools must have massive buildings and elaborate equipment, but are content with little, or adulterated truth. Jefferson and others dealing with big truths caught the idea of simple buildings. The loud cry will be ushered in by schools content with simple buildings and equipment, but they will be doing a great work.

11. Christian education is not content with only, learning things in the mind. What is studied must be put into practice. Manual training, is a part of every Christian school curriculum. The Papal system is content to have its students learn and hold the knowledge without making any practical application. Its students are ever learning, but never able to come to a knowledge of the truth. Manual training is not an essential part of their education. Before 1844, reformers in education established many manual training schools where students were taught agriculture, horticulture, gardening, various trades, such as blacksmithing, carpentry, manufacture of

cloth, printing, domestic science, dressmaking, care of the sick, etc. They were breaking away from the Papacy, and were coming "into the line of true education." Since the loud cry will find many schools that have carried these reforms farther, the results will be greater.

12. Christian training schools make provision for physical culture and healthful exercise by providing plenty of useful labor. Papal education makes little provision for manual training, therefore athletics, sports, games and gymnasiums become the artificial substitutes for God's plan for physical exercises. Schools preparing students for the loud cry should complete the work they have started.

13. Christian schools have for one of their most important objects the training of students to be self-governing, to take their places, not as dependent and devitalized members of the church, but as independent and original workers, under the direction of God's Spirit, all co-operating in harmony with divine principles. The Papal system makes no effort to train students to be self-governing, for such a training is fatal to the Papal church organization. Self-government appeared as an integral part of educational reform before 1844. Is it appearing in your school?

14. Every Christian missionary should be a producer. In other words, he should be self-supporting. No great religious movement can be started, or successfully carried forward, that has not an army of lay members who are active self-supporting missionaries. Christian schools have no greater object than to train such an army. Papal schools must avoid this, for it is destructive to their system of organization for controlling men. Christian schools before 1844 caught this idea of training missionaries for the midnight cry. Church leaders suppressed this reform. Christian schools before the loud cry will turn out an army of self-supporting workers.

15. The needy places of the world are calling for self-supporting missionaries. When the church opposed Oberlin's training missionaries, and refused to give them a place in the regular work, thousands of them went to the Indians, to the freedmen, to the mountain whites, and to foreign countries, under the direction of the American Missionary Society, an organization created by self-supporting workers.

16. Oberlin teachers, in order to make their school a success, sacrificed heavily in the matter of wages. Her students were encouraged to go where God called, with little concern over the question of remuneration. Oberlin considered it her duty as well as her pleasure to assist students to find their life work.

17. Oberlin teachers shortened the time students spent in school, and made their study practical by correlating class work with the reforms they desired their students to accept.

18. Opposition to Oberlin, while she was in the line of true education, brought to her friends and their means, and her attendance increased.

19. Outside opposition is a serious matter to a Christian school, but so long as the school keeps in "the line of true education," the opposition will only strengthen the reform. But long continued internal opposition is destructive. It was responsible for the downfall of the 16th century Reformation; it ruined the movement in 1844.

20. The spirit of a parent is necessary to the prosperity and continued success of educational reforms. Oberlin had this blessing in a marked degree. Consider the advantage of having one teacher, strong as a reformer, on a faculty for fifty years.

Students, are you doing all you can to bring your school "into the line of true education?"

5. Practical Subjects for the Curriculum

"The students are in our schools for a special training to become acquainted with all lines of work that should they go out as missionaries they could be self-reliant and able, through their educated ability, to furnish themselves with necessary conveniences and facilities." (*Testimonies for the Church*, Vol. 6, p. 208).

"Studies should generally be few and well chosen, and those who attend our colleges are to have a different training than that of the common schools of the day." (*Christian Education*, p. 47).

In addition to those subjects usually considered essential, we have the following which our schools should teach, so that the student, leaving the institution, is equipped not only to teach them to others, but to use them for his own support:—

Carpentry and building:—

"Under the guidance of experienced carpenters .... students themselves should erect buildings on the school grounds ... learning how to build economically." (*Testimonies for the Church*, Vol. 6, p. 176).

Agriculture, fruit raising, gardening:—

"Study in agricultural lines should be the A, B, C, of the education given in our schools... Small fruits should be planted, and vegetables and flowers cultivated... (Students) are to plant ... ornamental and fruit trees." (*Ibid.*, pp. 179, 181).

Various trades:—

"Preparation should be made for teaching blacksmithing, painting, shoemaking, cooking, baking, laundering, mending, typewriting and printing." (*Ibid.*, p. 182).

Stock and poultry raising:—

"Students have been taught ... to care wisely for cattle and poultry." ("An Appeal for the Madison School," p. 1).

Nursing:—

"Training for medical missionary work is one of the grandest objects for which any school can be established." (*Idem*).

Household duties:—

"Boys as well as girls should gain a knowledge of household duties.... To make a bed and put a room in order, to wash dishes, to prepare a meal, to wash and repair his own clothing, is a training that need not make any boy less manly... Let girls, in turn, learn to harness and drive a horse, and to use the saw and hammer as well as the rake and the hoe." (*Education*, p. 216).

Cooking and sewing:—

"There should have been experienced teachers to give lessons to young ladies in the cooking department. Young girls should have been instructed to manufacture wearing apparel, to cut, make and mend garments." (*Christian Education*, p. 19).

Self-supporting:—Students "have been learning to become self-supporting, and a training more important than this they could not receive" ("An Appeal for the Madison School," p. 1). "The lesson of self-help learned by the student would go far toward preserving institutions of learning from the burden of debt." (*Education*, p. 221).

Hand work:—There is a science in hand work which Christian educators must recognize. It is a brain developer as well as a way to physical support. Scientists have found that symmetrical mental development is impossible apart from this physical training, for by the use of the hand an important area of the brain is developed. Again, a time of trouble is ahead of us when those who are in "the line of true education" will not have access to machinery which is so common today, and much now done in factory and shop will of necessity be done by hand. But success in this as in every reform will be in proportion to one's love of the cause. The educator who spoke, of manual training as "hoehandle education" came from a school whose Board had provided facilities for teaching agriculture and various trades, but these had all been neglected. That teacher's attitude made the students feel that these important subjects were only secondary.

A changed program necessary:—Many of the subjects in the curriculum, the Lord has said, are not essential and should be weeded out.

These practical studies, he says, are essential, but they can not find their proper place by the side of the intellectual subjects until the program, followed for years and adapted to the old Order, is radically changed to meet the new demands. Again, it is necessary to make a number of radical reforms before a program can be arranged which gives students an opportunity to earn their school expenses while studying.

> "We need schools that will be self-supporting, and this can be if teachers and students will be helpful, industrious and economical." ("Words of Encouragement to Self-supporting Workers, p. 28 [Jan. 24, 1907]).

We must have schools of this character to train the missionaries that God calls for in the loud cry.

Schools of a new order:—

> "The plan of the schools we shall establish in these closing years of the work are to be of an entirely different order from those we have instituted... There is among us too much clinging to old customs; and because of this we are far behind where we should be in the development of the third angel's message. Because men could not comprehend the purpose of God in the plans laid before as for the education of workers, methods have been followed in some of our schools which have retarded rather than advanced the work of God." ("The Madison School," p. 29).

In the school with the new order of things we shall find that in addition to other essential studies,

> "The students have been taught to raise their own crops, to build their own houses, and to care wisely for cattle and poultry. They have been learning to become self-supporting, and a training more important than this they could not receive. Thus they have obtained a valuable education for usefulness in missionary fields.
>
> "To this is added the knowledge of how to treat the sick and to care for the injured. This training for medical missionary work is one of the grandest objects for which any school can be established. The educational work at the school and the sanitarium can go forward hand in hand. The instruction given at the school will benefit the patients, and the instruction given to the sanitarium patients will be a blessing to the school... The class of education given .... is such as will be accounted a treasure of great value by those who take up missionary work in foreign fields. If many more in other schools were receiving a similar training, we as a people would be a spectacle to the world, to angels,

and to men. The message would be quickly carried to every country, and souls now in darkness would be brought to the light.

"The time is soon coming when God's people, because of persecution, will be scattered in many countries. Those who have received an all-round education will have great advantage wherever they are. The Lord reveals divine wisdom in thus leading His people to train all their faculties and capabilities for the work of disseminating truth... You have no time to lose. Satan will soon rise up to create hindrances; let the work go forward while it may... Then the light of truth will be carried in a simple and effective way, and a great work will be accomplished for the Master in a short time... We are to learn to be content with simple food and clothing, that we may save much means to invest in the work of the gospel." ("An Appeal for the Madison School," p. 1-3).

There is hope:—It is your duty as students to seek to discover what God's plan is for our schools, and may this little history enable you to better understand the kind of education that existed in our older schools so that you may avoid it. Let me impress you again with the thought that you must seek God for help to keep you from having worldly yokes of education placed on your necks, even by your teachers. Remember that God has said these pointed words to us teachers and students:

"We are in positive danger of bringing into our educational work the customs and fashions that prevail in the schools of the world." ("The Madison School," p. 28).

We have spent years wandering in the wilderness of worldly education. If we lack faith and courage to enter into this reform, God will raise up men who will do it. Already we know of worldly educators who look with favor upon the plan of education that has been delivered to us. For instance, the present United States Commissioner of Education, Doctor P. P. Claxton, like Horace Mann of old, is in sympathy with it; and, after visiting a number of schools that are striving to work out these reforms, he expressed to a company of teachers his appreciation of the system of education in the following words:

"I wish very much it were possible for me to be present at the meeting of teachers and nurses of the hill schools which you are holding this week. I am greatly interested in the work which these schools are doing. The work which you are doing at Madison is remarkable and worthy of high praise. If you succeed permanently in maintaining the school on its present basis, it can not fail to accomplish great good.

The work which you are doing is highly practicable, and seems to me to be based on important fundamental principles of education. The same is true of the small schools which I visited, and I shall watch their progress with the greatest interest. I believe that you will succeed in accomplishing what you have in mind.

"All education must grow out of the life of the people educated. You and the teachers you are sending out are wisely recognizing this principle. In order to educate children, parents must be educated also. All real education must be education of the whole community, and it must take hold of the life which the people live, making them more intelligent about this life. It is difficult and practically impossible to attain better conditions until existing conditions are understood."

Have we the Caleb and Joshua spirit, and will we say, We are well able, by God's help, to build up a school "in the line of true education?" We must remember the promise that our schools "are prisoners of hope, and God will correct and enlighten them and bring them back to their upright position of distinction from the world." If we are willing and obedient, God will give us the victory we need.

"Let not managers, teachers or helpers swing back in their old customary way of letting their influence negative the very plans the Lord has presented as the best plan for the physical, mental and moral education of our youth. The Lord calls for steps in advance." (*Review and Herald*, Dec. 27, 1901).

"Teachers, trust in God, and go forward, "My grace is sufficient for you" is the assurance of the Great Teacher. Catch the inspiration of the words, and never, never talk doubt and unbelief. Be energetic. There is no half-and-half service in pure and undefiled religion." (*Fundamentals of Christian Education*, p. 436).

"Before we can carry the message of present truth in all its fullness to other countries, we must first break every yoke. We must come into the line of true education, walking in the wisdom of God, and not in the wisdom of the world. God calls for messengers who will be true reformers. We must educate, educate, to prepare a people who will understand the message, and then give the message to the world. ("The Madison School," p. 30).

"Now as never before we need to understand the true science of education. If we fail to understand this we shall never have a place in the kingdom of God."

APPENDIX

Appendix A — The Madison School

Ellen G. White

1908

Chapter 1—Encourage the Workers

Sanitarium, Cal.,

March 4, 1907.

I have been instructed that encouragement should be given to the work in the South, and that special help should come to the work in Nashville, Madison, and Huntsville.

At the school in Madison it has been necessary to work with the strictest economy in order that the educational work undertaken there might be carried forward. Let our brethren who have means remember this school and its needs.

A good work was done by Brethren Sutherland and Magan at Berrien Springs; in their labors at that place they went beyond their strength, imperiling their health, and even their lives. In their efforts at Madison, they are working too hard, and amid many difficulties. These brethren need not only our confidence, but also our help, that they may place the Madison school where it can accomplish the work that God designs it to do. I pray that the Lord will sanctify the understanding of our people, that these men may not be left to sacrifice their health in the work they are trying to do. I pray that teachers and students may have wisdom and courage to act well their part, and that they may be especially blessed in making the school a success.

It is impossible to make the Madison school what it should be, unless it is given a liberal share in the means that shall be appropriated for the work in the South. Will our brethren act their part in the spirit of Christ?

The South is to be especially favored now, because of the neglect of the past. The atonement for the failure of the past to meet the needs of this field, should be full and ample. The institutions in the South that for years should have stood on vantage-ground, are now to be especially favored. The Huntsville school must be encouraged to enlarge its work. Every possible advantage should be given to these schools, that they may show what can be done in making the earth to yield her treasures. The Madison and Huntsville schools are to be an object-lesson to the people in their vicinity.

I was shown that there is danger of these schools being circumscribed in their plans and limited in their advantages. This should not be. Everything possible should be done to encourage the students who need the class of instruction that can be given at these schools, that they may go forth properly instructed to do a work for others who need the same education and training that they have received. Fields are opening on every side to the work that such laborers could do.

For the work in and about Nashville, we should do all we can to put it on a solid basis. The work should be conducted with simplicity, and in a way that will recommend the truth. There are many places in the South open to our work; but by all means let us make a beginning in the important cities, and carry the message *now*. "For thus saith the Lord of hosts; Yet once, it is a little while, and I will shake the heavens, and the earth, and the sea, and the dry land; and I will shake all nations, and the Desire of all nations shall come: and I will fill this house with glory, saith the Lord of hosts."

CHAPTER 2—THE SEARCH FOR A SITE

On Steamer "Morning Star," on the
Cumberland River, June 13, 1904.

Elder A. G. Daniells,
Washington, D. C.,

Dear Brother Daniells,

We are returning from our trip up the river to look for land suitable for school work. We went from Nashville to Carthage, a distance of about one hundred and seventy miles by the river and seventy-eight miles by rail. We looked at several places; but the fertile land up the river is altogether too high in price for us to think of purchasing it for school purposes.

Tomorrow morning we shall reach Edgefield Junction, which is only twelve miles from Nashville. We shall stay there for the rest of the day; for we wish to visit a farm which is for sale at Madison, about nine miles from Nashville, and two and a half miles from the railway. It is said that this farm contains nearly one hundred acres of good bottom land, more than one hundred acres of second quality agricultural land suitable for grain and fruit, and about two hundred acres of pasture land. We think that it can be purchased for about twelve thousand dollars. It is said that there is on it over two thousand dollars' worth of stock and farm implements. I desire to look at this farm, and if it be the will of the Lord, I shall do so tomorrow afternoon. The farm has a roomy house, barns, and other buildings, and two and a half miles of good stone fence. Considering its advantages, its price is less than anything else we have seen in this part of Tennessee.

We should enter at once upon the establishment, in suitable places near Nashville, of a school for white people and a school for colored people. The workers in Nashville will gain influence from these working centers. The teachers in these schools can help the work in Nashville.

I have been instructed that the land on which our schools shall be established should be near enough to Nashville that there might be a connection between the schools and the workers in Nashville. Further than this, there are in Nashville large institutions for the education of the colored people, and our colored school is to be near enough to these institutions for the wing of their protection to be thrown over it. There is less inclination to oppress the colored people in this section of Tennessee than in many other parts of the South. Prejudice will not be so easily aroused. The institutions that have been established for the education of the colored people are richly endowed, and are in charge of white men. The presence of these institutions was one reason why Nashville was designated as the place in which the printing-office was to be established. I was instructed that the work in the South should have every advantage to print and publish books, that this work might gain a standing far ahead of that which it has had in the past.

Suggestions have been made by some that it might be well to sell our property in Huntsville, and move the school to some other place, but I have been instructed that this suggestion had its birth in unbelief. Our school in Huntsville is in a good location, and the large State Normal school for the training of colored teachers, which is carried on not far from there by those not of our faith, has created an influence in favor of educating the Negro, which our people should appreciate. We should have in Huntsville facilities for the education of a goodly number of students. We should have a primary school and a school for more advanced students. It would take years to build up in a new place the work that has already been done in Huntsville.

My soul is stirred within me as this matter is presented to me. I have not yet been to Huntsville, but I have an article written regarding what should be there in the future.

We must plan wisely. God will go before us if we will look to Him as our Counselor and our strength. We need to get away from our selfishness, and begin to work for the Lord in earnest.

CHAPTER 3—THE PURCHASE OF A PROPERTY

The property found at Madison, Tenn., was finally purchased as the site for the establishment of a training school for white workers. In an article published in the *Review and Herald*, Aug. 18, 1904, I gave a description of this property, and an outline of proposed plans to be carried out in the operation of the school, as follows:

In connection with the work in Nashville, I wish to speak of the school work that Brethren Sutherland and Magan are planning to do. I was surprised when, in speaking of the work they wished to do in the South, they spoke of establishing a school in some place a long way from Nashville. From the light given me, I knew that this would not be the right thing to do, and I told them so. The work that these brethren can do, because of the experience gained at Berrien Springs, is to be carried on within easy access of Nashville; for Nashville has not yet been worked as it should be. And it will be a great blessing to the workers in the school to be near enough to Nashville to be able to counsel with the workers there.

In searching for a place for the school, the brethren found a farm of four hundred acres for sale, about nine miles from Nashville. The size of the farm, its situation, the distance that it is from Nashville, and the moderate sum for which it could be purchased, seemed to point it out as the very place for the school work. We advised that this place be purchased. I knew that all the land would ultimately be needed. For the work of the students, and to provide homes for the teachers, such land can be used advantageously. And as our work advances, a portion of this tract may be required for a country sanitarium.

Other properties were examined, but we found nothing so well suited for our work. The price of the place, including standing crops, farm machinery, and over seventy head of cattle, was $12,723. It has been purchased, and as soon as possible, Brethren Magan and Sutherland, with a few experienced helpers, will begin school work there. We feel confident that the Lord has been guiding in this matter.

Proposed Plans

The plan upon which our brethren propose to work is to select some of the best and most substantial young men and women from Berrien Springs and other places in the North, who believe that God has called them to the work in the South, and give them a brief training as teachers.

Thorough instruction will be given in Bible study, physiology, and the history of our message; and special instruction in agriculture will be given. It is hoped that many of these students will eventually connect with schools in various places in the South. In connection with these schools there will be land that will be cultivated by teachers and students, and the proceeds from this work will be used for the support of the schools.

We went once more to see the farm, after its purchase had been completed, and were very much pleased with it. I earnestly hope that the school to be established there will be a success, and will help to build up the work of the Lord in that part of the vineyard. There are men of means in various parts of the land who can assist this enterprise by loans without interest, and by liberal gifts.

Let us sustain Brethren Sutherland and Magan in their efforts to advance this important work. They gained a valuable experience in Berrien Springs, and the providence of God has led them to feel that they must labor in the Southern field. God helped them constantly in their efforts at Berrien Springs, as they steadily advanced, determined that obstacles should not stop the work. They are not leaving Berrien Springs because of dissension or strife. They are not fleeing from duty. They are leaving a place where a school has been established, to go to a new field, where the work may be much harder. They have only means enough to pay part of the price of the land. They should not be left to struggle along misunderstood and unaided, at the sacrifice of health.

As these brethren go to the South to take hold of pioneer work in a difficult field, we ask our people to make their work as effective as possible by assisting them in the establishment of the new school near Nashville.

I ask our people to help the work in the Southern field by aiding Brethren Sutherland and Magan and their faithful associates in the carrying forward of the important enterprise they have undertaken. Brethren and sisters, the poverty and the needs of the Southern field call urgently for your assistance. There is a great work to be done in that field, and we ask you to act your part.

Chapter 4—A Country Sanitarium

Early in the history of the Madison school, it was suggested that a sanitarium might be established on a portion of the property purchased for the school farm. In letters written to those in charge of medical missionary work in the Southern States, I pointed out the advantages that are gained by establishing a training school and a sanitarium in close proximity. These letters were written in the fall of 1904, and, a year later, the principles set forth in this correspondence were incorporated in an article, and sent to the brethren assembled in a Medical Missionary Convention at College View, Neb., November 21-26, 1905.

The article is as follows:

Co-operation Between Schools and Sanitariums

I have been instructed that there are decided advantages to be gained by the establishment of a school and a sanitarium in close proximity, that they may be a help one to the other. Instruction regarding this was given to me when we were making decisions about the location of our buildings in Takoma Park. Whenever it is possible to have a school and a sanitarium near enough together for helpful co-operation between the two institutions, and yet separated sufficiently to prevent one from interfering with the work of the other, let them be located so as to carry on their work in conjunction. One institution will give influence and strength to the other; and, too, money can be saved by both institutions, because each can share the advantages of the other.

In connection with our larger schools there should be provided facilities for giving many students thorough instruction regarding gospel medical missionary work. This line of work is to be brought into our colleges and training-schools as a part of the regular instruction. This will make it unnecessary for our youth from all parts of the land to go to Battle Creek, or to any other one or two places, to obtain a thorough and satisfactory education and training.

Those in training to be nurses and physicians should daily be given instruction that will develop the highest motives for advancement. They should attend our colleges and training-schools; and the teachers in these institutions of learning should realize their responsibility to work with and pray with the students. In these schools, students should learn to be true medical missionaries, firmly bound up with the gospel ministry.

Our people who have a deep interest in the children and youth, and in the training of laborers to carry forward the work essential for this time, need not be left in perplexity and uncertainty about the steps to be taken for the training of their youth as medical missionaries. God will open ways before all who humbly seek Him for wisdom in the perfecting of Christian character. He will have places ready for them in which to begin to do genuine missionary work. It is to prepare laborers for this work that our schools and sanitariums are established.

For the strengthening of this line of effort, counsel has been given that in connection with our larger schools there should be established small sanitariums. Whenever a well-equipped sanitarium is located near a school, it may add greatly to the strength of the medical missionary course in the school, if the managers establish perfect co-operation between the two institutions. The teachers in the school can help the workers in the sanitarium by their advice and counsel, and by sometimes speaking to the patients. And, in return, those in charge of the sanitarium can assist in training for field service the students who are desirous of becoming medical missionaries. Circumstances, of course, must determine the details of the arrangements that it will be best to make. As the workers in each institution plan unselfishly to help one another, the blessing of the Lord will surely rest upon both institutions.

No one man, whether a teacher, a physician, or a minister, can ever hope to be a complete whole. God has given to every man certain gifts, and has ordained that men be associated in His service, in order that the varied talents of many minds may be blended. The contact of mind with mind tends to quicken thought and increase the capabilities. The deficiencies of one laborer are often made up by the special gifts of another; and as physicians and teachers thus associated unite in imparting their knowledge, the youth under their training will receive a symmetrical, well-balanced education for service.

In all these efforts, there will come many opportunities for manifesting gentlemanly courtesy. The Christian is always courteous. And by association with his fellow-workers, he becomes more and more refined. He learns to overlook little points of difference regarding questions that are of no vital consequence. Such a man, when in charge of one of the Lord's institutions, is willing to deny self and to yield his personal opinions on matters of minor importance, in order that, with all brotherly kindness, he may co-operate heartily with the managers of another institution near by. He will not hesitate to speak plainly and firmly when occasion demands; but his every word and act will be mingled with a courtesy so kindly, so Christlike, that no offense can be taken. Powerful is the influence for good that is exercised by a consecrated, active Christian gentleman. And when the managers of our institutions in close proximity learn to unite their forces, and to labor unselfishly and untiringly for the upbuilding of one another's work, the results for good are far-reaching.

The benefits of hearty co-operation extend beyond physicians and teachers, students and sanitarium helpers. When a sanitarium is built near a school, those in charge of the educational institution have a grand opportunity of setting a right example before those who all through life have been easy-going idlers, and who have come to the sanitarium for treatment. The patients will see the contrast between the idle, self-indulgent life that they have lived, and the life of self-denial and service lived by Christ's followers. They will learn that the object of medical missionary work is to restore, to correct wrongs, to show human beings how to avoid the self-indulgence that brings disease and death.

The words and actions of the workers in the sanitarium and in the school plainly reveal that life is an intensely solemn thing, in view of the account which all must render to God. Each one should now put his talents out to the exchangers, adding to the Master's gift, blessing others with the blessings given him. At the day of judgment, the life-work of each one is investigated, and each one receives a reward proportionate to his efforts.

That the best results may be secured by the establishment of a sanitarium near a school, there needs to be perfect harmony between the workers in both institutions. This is sometimes difficult to secure, especially when teachers and physicians are inclined to be self-centered, each considering as of the greatest importance the work with which he is most closely connected. When men who are self-confident are in charge of institutions in close proximity, great annoyance might result were each determined to carry out his own plans, refusing to make concessions to others. Both those at the head of the sanitarium and those at the head of the school will need to guard against clinging tenaciously to their own ideas concerning things that are really nonessentials.

There is a great work to be done by our sanitariums and schools. Time is short. What is done must be done quickly. Let those who are connected with these important instrumentalities be wholly converted. Let them not live for self, for worldly purposes, withholding themselves from full consecration to God's service. Let them give themselves, body, soul, and spirit, to God, to be used by Him in saving souls. They are not at liberty to do with themselves as they please; they belong to God; for He has bought them with the life-blood of His only-begotten Son. And as they learn to abide in Christ, there will remain in the heart no room for selfishness. In His service they will find the fullest satisfaction.

Let this be taught and lived by medical missionary workers. Let these laborers tell those with whom they come in contact that the life that men and women now live will one day be examined by a just God, and that each one must now do his best, offering to God consecrated service. Those in charge of the school are to teach the students to use for the highest, holiest purpose the talents God has given them, that they may accomplish the greatest good in this world. Students need to learn what it means to have a real aim in life, and to obtain an exalted understanding of what true education means. They need to learn what it means to be true gospel medical missionaries,—missionaries who can go forth to labor with the ministers of the Word in needy fields.

Wherever there is a favorable opportunity, let our sanitariums and our schools plan to be a help and a strength to each other. The Lord would have His work move forward solidly. Let light shine forth as God designed that it should from His institutions, and let God be glorified and honored. This is the purpose and plan of heaven in the establishment of these institutions. Let physicians and nurses and teachers and students walk humbly with God, trusting wholly in Him as the only One who can make their work a success.

November 14, 1905.

CHAPTER 5—LABORING IN UNITY AND IN FAITH

Sanitarium, Cal.,
October 15, 1906.

Dear Brethren,

Among brethren engaged in various lines of the Lord's work there should ever be seen a desire to encourage and strengthen one another. The Lord is not pleased with the course of those who make the way difficult for some who are doing a work appointed to them by the Master. If these critics were placed in the position of those whom they criticize, they would desire far different treatment from that which they give their brethren.

We are to respect the light that led Brethren Magan and Sutherland to purchase property and establish the school at Madison. Let no one speak words that would tend to demerit their work, or to divert students from the school. I do not charge any one with an intention to do wrong, but from the light I have received, I can say that there is danger that some will criticize unjustly the work of our brethren and sisters connected with the school at Madison. Let every encouragement possible be given to those who are engaged in an effort to give to children and youth an education in the knowledge of God and of His law.

To the workers in Madison I would say, Be of good courage. Do not lose faith. Your heavenly Father has not left you to achieve success by your own endeavors. Trust in Him, and He will work in your behalf. It is your privilege to experience and to demonstrate the blessings that come through walking by faith and not by sight. Work with an eye single to the glory of God. Make the most of your capabilities, and you will increase in knowledge. Those who do the will of God may be permitted to pass through suffering, but the Lord will cause them to triumph at last.

The Lord has helped you in the selection of the location for the school, and as you continue to work under the guidance of the Holy Spirit, your efforts will be successful. The Lord will give you spirit and life, if you will not permit yourselves to become discouraged. We trust that from your brethren you may receive the help of harmonious action, of prayers, and of means. But let not one feeling of discouragement be cherished. The Lord has a work for you to do where you are, and those who are doing His work need never be discouraged.

Sanitarium, Cal.,
October 30, 1906.

Dear Brother _____,

The school at Madison must be treated fairly, yes, right loyally. If all will act a part to help this school, the Lord will bless them. I am determined to act my part. I have not lost one jot of my interest in the Southern field. I want to act a part in helping all lines of the work.

Let us take all these burdens to the Lord God of Israel. Let us work in His name and for His glory. Our hearts need to be filled with sympathy. We need to have courage and joy in the Lord. Never, never let words be spoken that will make the burden weigh heavier upon those who have struggled for so long to carry out the expressed will and purpose of God. I fully believe that those who are connected with the school at Madison are carrying out the will of God. I believe that this farm is the very place for the school. Provision must be made to aid this institution. Those who are struggling to establish this school must be helped.

The Lord is good; let us trust in Him. I do love the Lord, but it makes my heart ache to see and feel the magnitude of the necessities that must be met. We will say, The Lord lives, and He is rich in resources. Let us have thankful hearts, and be of good courage in the Lord. Keeping our eyes fixed on Jesus, we may triumph in Him.

November 6, 1906.

The case of the Madison school, and the good work that should be done there without let or hindrance has been placed before me, and I designed that this sum of money, though only a small amount in comparison with what they actually need, should be invested in that enterprise. I could not feel at rest in my mind until this was done. The workers there could use double this amount with good results. It has been presented to me that before this our people should have provided this school with means, and thus placed it on vantage-ground. This is the way in which I still view the matter.

Brethren _____ and _____ are men in whom I have confidence. I encouraged the purchasing of the farm on which the Madison school is established. Had it been still farther from Nashville, this would have been no objection. It is well situated, and will produce its treasures. Those who are carrying on the work of this school need and should have encouragement. The brethren bearing responsibilities of a different character in some respects should give freedom to those who have as good judgment as they themselves have in regard to what is needed on the farm in buildings for sanitarium and school purposes.

The Madison school farm is to be an object-lesson for the Southern field. It is in an excellent location, and fully as near Nashville as it should be.

Sanitarium, Cal.,

January 19, 1907.

Elder _____,

Dear Brother,

Today I have been carrying a heavy burden on my heart. Last night some matters of special importance were opened up before me. I seemed to be passing through a severe conflict. I was addressing a company of men and women, and presenting to them the dangers of our people. I spoke of our great need of being much with God in prayer. I had words of encouragement to give to different ones.

Words of instruction were given me to speak to you and Elders _____, _____, and _____. I said: You have a work to do to encourage the school work in Madison, Tennessee. There are but few teachers among us who have had experience in carrying forward the work in hard places. The workers who have been striving to carry out the mind and will of God in Madison have not received the encouragement they should have. Unless Brother Sutherland is relieved of some of the pressure that is upon him, he will fall under the burden.

You may ask, What is needed? I answer, It is encouragement. Brethren Sutherland and Magan have had a severe lesson in the past. The Lord sent them correction and instruction, and they received the message from the Lord, and made confession....

When I was in Washington (August, 1904), I entreated Brethren Sutherland and Magan to believe that God had forgiven their mistakes, and I have since tried by my help and encouragement to have them realize that the Lord had placed them on vantage-ground.

It is your privilege, Brother _____, and the privilege of those who have wide influence in the work, to let these brethren understand that they have your confidence and encouragement in the work they are bravely doing. Brother Sutherland is in a precarious state of health. We can not afford to lose him; we need his experience in the school work. The brethren who have influence should do all in their power to hold up the hands of these workers by encouraging and supporting the work of the Madison school. Means should be appropriated to the needs of the work in Madison, that the labors of the teachers may not be so hard in the future.

CHAPTER 6—LETTER TO A CONFERENCE PRESIDENT

Sanitarium, Cal.,
February 5, 1907.

Dear Brother,

I write to ask you to interest yourself in the school at Madison. Brethren Sutherland and Magan have worked diligently, far beyond their strength, to open up the school work in this place, which is of the Lord's appointment. They have endeavored to establish a school that would fit young men and young women to act as missionaries in the Southern field.

At the present time they should have five thousand dollars to enable them to provide suitable facilities for the work, and still more should be provided, in order that a small sanitarium may be connected with the school.

So far they have received very little help in this enterprise, compared with the needs and importance of the work. They have worked hard, and have laid plans for such an education as is essential to prepare workers to teach the ignorant, and to explain the Scriptures. Besides the study of books, the students are taught to till the soil, to build houses, and to perform other useful labor.

The location of the Madison school is excellent, and possesses great advantages for school work. But the leaders in this work are carrying too heavy a burden, and should be relieved from the great anxiety that has rested upon them, because of a lack of means with which to do what must be done to provide suitable conditions for a successful school.

Shall we allow these workers to be burdened beyond their strength, carrying forward almost alone a work in which they should receive the hearty co-operation of their brethren?

I appeal to our brethren in _____ to help in this emergency, and make a liberal gift to the Madison school, that they may erect a chapel and school building. Such a building should have been provided for them long ago. Let us not leave these men to work under present disadvantages, when time is so precious, and the need for trained workers in the South is so great.

The work in the South has been sadly neglected. It is high time that our churches were awakened to their duty to this needy field. The light must shine forth amid the moral darkness of ignorance and superstition. The truth in its simplicity must be brought to those who are in ignorance.

In the common schools some things are taught that are a hindrance rather than a blessing. We need schools where the word of God is made the basis of education. The Madison training-school for teachers should have the hearty support of God's people. Therefore I ask you and your associates on the conference committee to act liberally in helping our brethren in Madison in this important work.

CHAPTER 7—LETTER TO THE SOUTHERN UNION CONFERENCE COMMITTEE

Sanitarium, Cal.,

February 24, 1907.

Dear Brethren,

I have a message to bear to our people in the Southern field. There is an important work to be carried forward in Nashville and vicinity, and a decided interest should be manifested in this field.

It is in harmony with the leadings of God's Spirit that Brethren Sutherland and Magan and their associates have begun a work at Madison. The Lord guided them in the selection of a location for the school. Had a small sanitarium been established in connection with the school, this would have been in the order of God; and these two institutions would have been a mutual help. This has not yet been done, but our brethren in Madison need not be discouraged.

I would say to our brethren in the Southern field, Let there be no restriction laid on the Madison school to limit its work in the field of its operation. If Brethren Sutherland and Magan have promised not to draw students to their school from the Southern States, they should be freed from any such restriction. Such a promise should never have been asked or granted. I am instructed to say that there should be no restrictions limiting their freedom to draw students from the Southern field. There is need of such an institution as has been established near Nashville, and let not one endeavor to hinder the attendance of those who can at that school best receive the training that will fit them to labor in the Southern States, and in other mission fields.

At Berrien Springs Brethren Sutherland and Magan carried on a work of self-sacrifice. They did not leave the North because they had lost their influence, they went to the South because they saw the needs of that field. In their work at Madison they should have encouragement from those whom they have come to help. Those who have in charge the disbursement of funds coming to the Southern field, should not fail to render proportionate aid to the Madison school.

In the Madison school the students are taught how to till the soil, how to build houses, and to perform other lines of useful labor. These are some of the lines of work that the Lord instructed us to introduce into our school in Australia. With a practical training, students will be prepared to fill useful positions in many places.

Skill in the common arts is a gift from God. He provides both the gift, and the wisdom to use the gift aright. When He desired a work done on the tabernacle, He said, "See, I have called by name Bezaleel the son of Uri, the son of Hur, of the tribe of Judah; and I have filled him with the Spirit of God, in wisdom, and in understanding, and in knowledge, and in all manner or workmanship."

Through the prophet Isaiah the Lord says: "Give ye ear, and hear My voice; hearken, and hear My speech. Doth the plowman plow all day to sow? doth he open and break the clods of his ground? When he hath made plain the face thereof, doth he not cast abroad the fitches, and scatter the cummin, and cast in the principal wheat and the appointed barley and the rye in their place? For his God doth instruct him to discretion, and doth teach him.

"For the fitches are not threshed with a threshing instrument, neither is a cart-wheel turned about upon the cummin; but the fitches are beaten out with a staff, and the cummin with a rod. Bread corn is bruised; because he will not ever be threshing it, nor break it with the wheel of his cart, nor bruise it with his horsemen. This also cometh forth from the Lord of hosts, which is wonderful in counsel, and excellent in working."

Today the Lord has definitely called some to the work of teaching others, to fit them for service in His cause. Let those who are so called go cheerfully to their field of labor, following ever the leadings of God.

God dispenses His gifts as it pleases Him. He bestows one gift upon one, and another gift upon another, but all for the good of the whole body. It is in God's order that some shall be of service in one line of work, and others in other lines,—all working under the self-same Spirit. The recognition of this plan will be a safeguard against carnal emulation, pride, envy, or contempt of one another. It will strengthen unity and mutual love.

If in the opening providence of God, it becomes necessary to erect a meeting-house in some locality, the Lord is pleased if there are among His own people those to whom He has given wisdom and skill to perform the necessary work. He sends men to carry His truth to people of a strange tongue, and He has sometimes opened the minds of His missionaries, enabling them quickly to learn the language. The very ones whom they have come to help spiritually, will be a help to them in learning the language. By this relation the natives are prepared to hear the gospel message when it is given in their own tongue.

Chapter 8—A Missionary Education

In the work of soul-saving, the Lord calls together laborers who have different plans and ideas and various methods of labor. But with this diversity of minds, there is to be revealed a unity of purpose. Oftentimes in the past the work which the Lord designed should prosper has been hindered because men have tried to place a yoke upon their fellow workers who did not follow the methods which they supposed to be the best.

No exact pattern can be given for the establishment of schools in new fields. The climate, the surroundings, the condition of the country, and the means at hand with which to work, must all bear a part in shaping the work. The blessings of an all-around education will bring success in Christian missionary work. Through its means souls will be converted to the truth.

"Ye are the light of the world," Christ declares. "Let your light so shine before men, that they may see your good works, and glorify your Father which is in heaven." God's work in the earth in these last days is to reflect the light that Christ brought into the world. This light is to dissipate the gross darkness of ages. Men and women in heathen darkness are to be reached by those who at one time were in a similar condition of ignorance, but who have received the knowledge of the truth of God's word. These heathen nations will accept eagerly the instruction given them in a knowledge of God.

Very precious to God is His work in the earth. Christ and heavenly angels are watching it every moment. As we draw near to the coming of Christ, more and still more of missionary work will engage our efforts. The message of the renewing power of God's grace will be carried to every country and clime, until the truth shall belt the world. Of the number of them that shall be sealed will be those who have come from every nation and kindred and tongue and people. From every country will be gathered men and women who will stand before the throne of God and before the Lamb, crying, "Salvation unto our God which sitteth upon the throne, and unto the Lamb." But before this work can be accomplished, we must experience right here in our own country the work of the Holy Spirit upon our hearts.

God has revealed to me that we are in positive danger of bringing into our educational work the customs and fashions that prevail in the schools of the world. If teachers are not guarded in their work, they will place on the necks of their students worldly yokes instead of the yoke of Christ. The plan of the schools we shall establish in these closing years of the work is to be of an entirely different order from those we have instituted in the past.

For this reason, God bids us establish schools away from the cities, where, without let or hindrance, we can carry on the work of education upon plans that are in harmony with the solemn message that is committed to us for the world. Such an education as this can best be worked out where there is land to cultivate, and where the physical exercise taken by the students can be of such a nature as to act a valuable part in their character-building, and to fit them for usefulness in the fields to which they shall go.

God will bless the work of those schools that are conducted according to His design. When we were laboring to establish the educational work in Australia, the Lord revealed to us that this school must not pattern after any schools that had been established in the past. This was to be a sample school. The school was organized on the plan that God had given us, and He has prospered its work.

I have been shown that in our educational work we are not to follow the methods that have been adopted in our older established schools. There is among us too much clinging to old customs, and because of this we are far behind where we should be in the development of the third angel's message. Because men could not comprehend the purpose of God in the plans laid before us for the education of the workers, methods have been followed in some of our schools which have retarded rather than advanced the work of God. Years have passed into eternity with small results that might have shown the accomplishment of a great work. If the Lord's will had been done by the workers in earth as the angels do it in heaven, much that now remains to be done, would be already accomplished, and noble results would be seen as the fruit of missionary effort.

The usefulness learned on the school farm is the very education that is most essential for those who go out as missionaries to many foreign fields. If this training is given with the glory of God in view, great results will be seen. No work will be more effectual than that done by those who, having obtained an education in practical life, go forth to mission fields with the message of truth, prepared to instruct as they have been instructed. The knowledge they have obtained in the tilling of the soil and other lines of manual work, and which they carry with them to their fields of labor, will make them a blessing even in heathen lands.

Before we can carry the message of present truth in all its fullness to other countries, we must first break every yoke. We must come into the line of true education, walking in the wisdom of God, and not in the wisdom of the world. God calls for messengers who will be true reformers. We must educate, educate, to prepare a people who will understand the message, and then give the message to the world..

There has been a decided failure to meet the requirements of God in the Southern field. We need to ask the Lord to give us understanding that we may see our lack, and take in the situation in the South, and the need of doing the missionary work that lies right at hand. The uneducated people of the South need the knowledge of the gospel just as verily as do the heathen in far-off lands. God requires us to study how we may reach the neglected classes of the white and the colored people in the South, and with all the skill we can gain, to work for the souls of these men and women.

The Madison School

It was quite a problem with Brethren Sutherland and Magan and their faithful associates as to how, with limited means, they were to adapt themselves to the work in Madison, Tenn. They had many obstacles and difficulties to meet, some of which need never have come into the work.

The reason these brethren were persuaded to purchase the place now occupied by the Madison school, was because special light was given to me that this place was well adapted for the educational work that was most needed there. It was presented to me that this was a place where an all-round education could be given advantageously to students who should come from the North and the South for instruction. In what has already been accomplished by the Madison school, the Lord is making it manifest that He is blessing the work carried forward there, and is leading the teachers who are associated together in bearing the burdens of the work.

Many obstacles have been placed in the way of the pioneers at the Madison school of a nature to discourage them and drive them from the field. These obstacles were not placed there by the Lord. In some things the finite planning and devisings of men have worked counter to the work of God.

Let us be careful, brethren, lest we counterwork and hinder the progress of others, and so delay the sending forth of the gospel message. This has been done, and this is why I am now compelled to speak so plainly. If proper aid had been given to the school enterprise at Madison, its work might now be in a far more advanced stage of development. The work at Madison has made slow advancement, and yet, in spite of the obstacles and hindrances, these workers have not failed nor become discouraged; and they have been enabled to accomplish a good work in the cause of God.

The Lord does not set limits about His workers in some lines as men are wont to set. In their work, Brethren Magan and Sutherland have been hindered unnecessarily. Means have been withheld from them because in the organization and management of the Madison school, it was not placed under the control of the conference. But the reasons why this school was not owned and controlled by the conference have not been duly considered.

The lack of interest in this work, by some who should have valued it highly, is decidedly wrong. Our brethren must guard themselves against the repetition of such experiences.

The Lord does not require that the educational work at Madison shall be changed all about before it can receive the hearty support of our people. The work that has been done there is approved of God, and He forbids that this line of work shall be broken up. The Lord will continue to bless and sustain the workers so long as they follow His counsel.

Brethren Sutherland and Magan are as verily set to do the work of the Lord at Madison as other workers are appointed to do their part in the cause of present truth. The light given me is that we should help these brethren and their associates, who have worked beyond their strength, under great disadvantages. Let us seek to understand the situation, and see that justice and mercy are not forgotten in the distribution of funds.

The leaders in the work of the Madison school are laborers together with God. More must be done in their behalf by their brethren. The Lord's money is to sustain them in their labors. They have a right to share the means given to the cause. They should be given a proportionate share of the means that comes in for the furtherance of the cause.

June 18, 1907.

Ellen G. White

Appendix B — An Appeal for the Madison School

Ellen G. White

1908

I am acquainted with the necessities of the work being done by Brethren Magan and Sutherland and their co-laborers at Madison, Tennessee, for the Lord has presented this matter clearly before me.

Light had been given that a great work was to be done in and around Nashville. When these brethren were looking for a location for their school, they found the farm where the school is now established. The price was moderate, and the advantages were many. I was shown that the property should be secured for the school, and advised them to look no farther.

The Character of the Work

The school at Madison not only educates in a knowledge of the Scriptures, but it gives a practical training that fits the student to go forth as a self-supporting missionary to the field to which he is called. In their work at Madison, Brethren Sutherland and Magan and their associates have borne trial nobly. The students have been taught to raise their own crops, to build their own houses, and to care wisely for cattle and poultry. They have been learning to become self-supporting, and a training more important than this they could not receive. Thus they have obtained a valuable education for usefulness in missionary fields.

To this is added the knowledge of how to treat the sick and to care for the injured. This training for medical missionary work is one of the grandest objects for which any school can be established.

THE NEED FOR A SANITARIUM

There are many suffering from disease and injury, who, when relieved of pain, will be prepared to listen to the truth. Our Saviour was a mighty Healer. In His name there may be many miracles wrought in the South and in other fields, through the instrumentality of the trained medical missionary.

It is essential that there shall be a sanitarium connected with the Madison school. The educational work at the school and the sanitarium can go forward hand in hand. The instruction given at the school will benefit the patients, and the instruction given to the sanitarium patients will be a blessing to the school.

THE VALUE OF AN ALL-ROUND EDUCATION

The class of education given at the Madison school is such as will be accounted a treasure of great value by those who take up missionary work in foreign fields. If many more in other schools were receiving a similar training, we as a people would be a spectacle to the world, to angels, and to men. The message would be quickly carried to every country, and souls now in darkness would be brought to the light.

It would have been pleasing to God if, while the Madison school has been doing its work, other such schools had been established in different parts of the Southern field. There is plenty of land lying waste in the South that might have been improved as the land about the Madison school has been improved. The time is soon coming when God's people, because of persecution, will be scattered in many countries. Those who have received as all-round education will have a great advantage wherever they are. The Lord reveals divine wisdom in thus leading His people to train all their faculties and capabilities for the work of disseminating truth.

A CALL TO SELF-DENIAL

Every possible means should be devised to establish schools of the Madison order in various parts of the South; and those who lend their means and their influence to help this work, are aiding the cause of God.

I am instructed to say to those who have means to spare: Help the work at Madison. You have no time to lose. Satan will soon rise up to create hindrances; let the work go forward while it may.

Let us strengthen this company of educators to continue the good work in which they are engaged, and labor to encourage others to do a similar work. Then the light of truth will be carried in a simple and effective way, and a great work will be accomplished for the Master in a short time.

When the Lord favors any of His servants with worldly advantages, it is that they may use those advantages for the benefit of others. We are to learn to be content with simple food and clothing, that we may save much means to invest in the work of the gospel.

Our lack of self-denial, our refusal to see the necessities of the cause for this time, and to respond to them, call for repentance and humiliation before God. It is a sin for one who knows the truth of God to fold his hands and leave his work for another to do. The gospel of Christ calls for entire consecration. Let our church-members now arise to their responsibilities and privileges. Let them spend less on self-indulgence and needless adorning. The money thus expended is the Lord's, and is needed to do a sacred work in His cause. Educate the children to do missionary work, and to bring their offerings to God. Let us awake to the spiritual character of the work in which we are engaged. This is no time for weakness to be woven into our experience.

THE WORK AT MADISON NOT TO BE HINDERED

The workers at Madison have devised and planned and sacrificed in order to carry the school there on right lines, but the work has been greatly delayed. The Lord guided in the selection of the farm at Madison, and He desires it to be managed on right lines, that others, learning from the workers there, may take up a similar work, and conduct it in a like manner.

In the work being done at the training-school for home and foreign missionary teachers in Madison, Tennessee, and in the small schools established by the teachers who have gone forth from Madison, we have an illustration of one way in which the message should be carried in many, many places.

Brethren Sutherland and Magan should be encouraged to solicit means for the support of their work. It is the privilege of these brethren to receive gifts from any of the people whom the Lord impresses to help. They should have means—God's means with which to work. The Madison enterprise has been crippled in the past, but now it must go forward. If this work had been regarded in the right light, and had been given the help it needed, we should long ere this have had a prosperous work at Madison. Our people are to be encouraged to give of their means to this work which is preparing students in a sensible and creditable way to go forth into neglected fields to proclaim the soon coming of Christ.

Now a modest sanitarium is being erected, and a more commodious school-building. These are necessary to carry on aright the work of education. In the past, Brethren Sutherland and Magan have used their tact and ability in raising means for the good of the cause as a whole. Now the time has come when these faithful workers should receive from their brethren, the Lord's stewards, the means that they need to carry on successfully the work of the Madison school and the little Madison sanitarium.

I appeal to our brethren to whom the Lord has entrusted the talent of means: Will you not help the workers at Madison, who have been instrumental in raising means for many enterprises? As the Lord's messenger, I ask you to help the Madison school now. This is its time of need. The money which you possess is the Lord's entrusted capital. It should be held in readiness to answer the calls in places where the Lord has need of it.

The necessities of the Madison school call for immediate help. Brethren, work while the day lasts; for the night cometh, when no man can work.

May 25, 1908.
Ellen G. White

Appendix C — The Work of the Madison School

Ellen G. White

1908

In the work being done at the training school for home and foreign missionary teachers in Madison, Tennessee, and in the small schools established by the teachers who have gone forth from Madison, we have an illustration of a way in which the message should be carried. I would say to the workers there, Continue to learn of Christ. Do not be daunted. Be free in the Lord; be free. Much acceptable work has been done in Madison. The Lord says to you, Go forward. Your school is to be an example of how Bible study, general education, physical education, and sanitarium work may be combined in many smaller schools that shall be established in simplicity in many places in the Southern states.

My brethren in responsible places, mourn not over the work that is being done at Madison to train workers to go forth into the highways and the hedges. It is the will of God that this work should be done. Let us cease to criticize the servants of God, and humble our own hearts before the Lord. Let us strengthen this company to continue the good work in which they are engaged, and labor to encourage others to do a similar work. Then the light of truth will be carried in a simple and effective way, and a great work will be accomplished for the Master in a short time.

When the Lord favors any of his servants with worldly advantages, it is that they may use those advantages for the benefit of the work. As laborers together with God, men are to keep constantly in mind the need of giving the message of Christ's soon coming to the people who have not been warned. In this we are not left to human intelligence alone, for angels of God are waiting to encourage us in a life of patience and self-denial. We are to learn to be content with simple food and clothing, that we may save much to be invested in the work of the gospel.

The gospel of Christ calls for entire consecration. The Christian sower is to go forth to sow. But many by their fretting and contentions are disqualifying themselves for labor. Their sluggish senses do not discern how feeble are their efforts, and how strong is their unbelief. Let our church members now arise to their responsibilities and privileges. Let them spend less on self-indulgence and needless adorning. The money thus expended is the Lord's, and is needed to do a sacred work in his cause. Educate the children to do missionary work, and to bring their offerings to God. Let us awake to our need of denying self. Let us awake to a sense of the spiritual character of the work in which we profess to be engaged.

I have said only a little in comparison with what might be said on this subject. But I call on our ministers, our teachers, and our physicians to awake out of sleep, and see the opportunities for work that are within their reach, but which for years have been allowed to pass unimproved.

Our lack of self-denial, our refusal to see the necessities of the cause at this time, and to respond to them, call for repentance and humiliation of heart before God. It is a sin for one who knows the truth of God to fold his hands and transfer his duty to another.

It is a sin for any to criticize and find fault with those who in their manner of working do not exactly meet their mind. Let none blame or censure the men who have labored at Madison. In the place of complaining at your brother's work, take up your own neglected work. Instead of picking flaws in your brother's character, search your own heart, confess your sins, and act honestly with God. Let there be condemnation of self for the work that lies undone all about you. Instead of placing impediments in the way of those who are trying to accomplish something in the South, let our eyes be opened to see that time is passing, and that there is much for you to do.

The Lord works through various agencies. If there are those who desire to step into new fields and take up new lines of labor, encourage them to do so. Seventh-day Adventists are doing a great and good work; let no man's hand be raised to hinder his brother. Those who have had experience in the work of God should be encouraged to follow the guidance and counsel of the Lord.

Do not worry lest some means shall go direct to those who are trying to do missionary work in a quiet and effective way. All the means is not to be handled by one agency or organization. There is much business to be done conscientiously for the cause of God. Help is to be sought from every possible source. There are men who can do the work of securing means for the cause, and when these are acting conscientiously and in harmony with the counsels of their fellow-laborers in the field which they represent, the hand of restraint is not to be laid upon them. They are surely laborers together with Him who gave his life for the salvation of souls.

Brethren Sutherland and Magan should be encouraged to solicit means for the support of their work. It is the privilege of these brethren to receive gifts from any of our people whom the Lord impresses to help. They should have means—God's means—with which to work. The Madison enterprise has been crippled in the past, but now it must go forward. If this work had been regarded in the right light, and had been given the help it needed, we should long ere this have had a prosperous work at Madison. Our people are to be encouraged to give of their means to this work which is preparing students in a sensible and creditable way to go forth into neglected fields to proclaim the soon coming of Christ.

The Lord directed Brethren Sutherland and Magan, as men of sound principles, to establish a work in the South. They have devised and planned and sacrificed in order to carry forward the work on right lines, but the work has been greatly delayed. The Lord guided his servants in the selection of the farm at Madison, and he desires that it be managed on right lines, that others, learning from the workers there, might take up a similar work and conduct it in a like manner. Brethren Sutherland and Magan are chosen of God and faithful, and the Lord of heaven says of them, I have a special work for these men to do at Madison, a work of educating and training young men and women for mission fields. The Spirit of the Lord will be with his workers if they will walk humbly before him. He had not bound about and restricted the labors of these self-denying, self-sacrificing men.

To those in our conferences who have felt that they had authority to forbid the gathering of means in certain territory I now say: This matter has been presented to me again and again. I now bear my testimony in the name of the Lord to those whom it concerns. Wherever you are, withhold your forbiddings. The work of God is not to be thus trammeled. God is being faithfully served by these men whom you have been watching and criticizing. They fear and honor the Lord; they are laborers together with Him. God forbids you to put any yokes on the necks of his servants. It is the privilege of these workers to accept gifts or loans that they may invest them to help in doing an important work that greatly needs to be done. This wonderful burden of responsibility which some suppose God has placed upon them with their official position, has never been laid upon them. If men were standing free on the high platform of truth, they would never accept the responsibility to frame rules and regulations that hinder and cramp God's chosen laborers in their work for the training of missionaries. When they learn the lesson that "All ye are brethren", and realize that their fellow-workers may know just as well as they how to use in the wisest way the talents and capabilities entrusted to them, they will remove the yokes that are now binding their brethren, and will give them credit for having love for souls and a desire to labor unselfishly to promote the interests of the cause.

Appendix D — Words of Encouragement to Self-Supporting Workers

Ellen G. White

1909

Report of a talk by Mrs. E. G. White to the teachers and students of the Nashville Agricultural and Normal Institute at Madison, Tenn., April 26, 1909

Schools for the Highways and Hedges

I am very glad to have the opportunity of speaking to as many as I see before me at this time, in a field where a large work is yet to be done. In all these unworked fields, special efforts are to be made. In laboring for the unwarned, we are to seek to "compel them to come in." Why?— Because souls are at stake. There is a message to be given to these souls, and those in the highways and in the hedges must hear the Word of life.

Several years ago, during a former visit to the South, while out on long drives, I sometimes asked who occupied the homes we passed, and I learned that in many of the larger Southern houses were men who bear important responsibilities in the care of great estates. Upon further inquiry, I learned that no one had sought to bring before these men the Word of life. None had gone to them, with Bible in hand, and said, "We have something precious for you, and we want that you should hear it." Now it has been presented before me repeatedly that this is a line of work that must be done. We are to go out into the highways and into the hedges, and carry to the people the message of truth that Christ has given us. We are to compel many to come in.

Christ meant much when he said, Go out into the highways and the hedges. You must not neglect the highways. You must bring the truth before those in the highways. Neither are you to neglect those that are in the hedges. In addition to the work that must be done in the great cities, there is a work to be performed for those that are scattered all through the regions round about. And how can we reach them?—One important means of accomplishing this work, is found in the establishment of small schools in needy communities. Even if there are but a few persons in a place, some means of reaching them should be devised. Once let the missionary spirit take hold of men and women, young and old, and we shall see many going into the highways and the hedges, and compelling the honest in heart to come in.

Some one may inquire, "How will you compel them?"—Let the truth of God, in its purity and power, be brought to bear upon the conscience of living agents, and let them be taught the preciousness of this truth. Let them realize that the Word of life, even Christ himself, came to our world because of God's desire to save fallen humanity; for "God so loved the world, that he gave his only begotten Son, that whosoever believeth in him should not perish, but have everlasting life."

THE MADISON SCHOOL TRAINS TEACHERS FOR THE HIGHLAND SCHOOLS AND FAMILY MISSION SCHOOLS

Nearly five years ago, when we were searching for a site on which to locate a training-school near Nashville, we visited this plantation that was afterwards secured; and I remember that when we first saw the place, we planned to go over it in carriages, some in one direction, and some in another, and we looked to God to impress our minds as to whether this were the place he wished us to choose for a training-center. For a time, the prospect looked forbidding; nevertheless, the plantation was secured, and the work was begun. The Lord would have the influence of this school widely extended by means of the establishment of small mission schools in needy settlements in the hills, where consecrated teachers may open the Scriptures to hungry souls, and let the light of life shine forth to those that are in darkness.

This is the very work that Christ did. He traveled from place to place, and labored for souls. And who was he?—The One equal with the Father. The Lord Jesus has set us an example. As you engage in school work in these needy communities, do not let any man come in to discourage you by saying, "Why do you spend your time in this way? Why not do a larger and more important work in a broader field?" Some, it is true, must plan to look forward to the time when they will do a large work in response to general calls; but who will attend to the highways? Who will go into the hedges? There are those that Christ will move upon, and they will see the necessity of entering neglected portions of the vineyard. They will delight to open the Scriptures to those that are in darkness and do not understand the truth. This is the very work that is to be done. Let every one of us stand in our lot and in our place. And if there are those whom the Lord moves upon to give themselves to the neglected portions of the vineyard, let no man seek to turn them away from their appointed work. If those who know the truth, conceal from others the great light that has shined into their own hearts, they are held accountable for neglecting their duty.

We feel an earnest interest in these schools. There is a wide field before us in the establishment of family mission schools. Let those who feel the burden of souls resting upon them, go out and do house-to-house work, and teach the people precept upon precept, here a little, and there a little, gradually leading them into the full light of Bible truth. This is what we had to do in the early days of the message. As earnest efforts are put forth, the Lord will let his blessing rest upon the workers, and rest upon those who are seeking for an understanding of the truth as it is in the Word of God.

There are precious truths, glorious truths, in God's Word, and it is our privilege to bring these truths before the people. In those parts of the field where many cannot attend meetings far away from their homes, we can bring the truth, to them personally, and can work with them in simplicity.

A Place for Old and Young in the Southern Field

In preparation for the coming of our Lord, we are to do a large work in the great cities. We have a solemn testimony to bear in these great centers. But in our planning for the extension of the work, far more than the cities alone, must be comprehended. In out-of-the-way places are many, many families that need to be looked after in order to learn whether they understand the work that Jesus is doing for his people. Those in the highways are not to be neglected, neither are those in the hedges; and as we journey about from place to place, and pass by house after house, we should often inquire, "Have the people who are living in these places, heard the message? Has the truth of God's Word been brought to their ears? Do they understand that the end of all things is at hand, and that the judgments of God are impending? Do they realize that every soul has been bought with an infinite price?" As I meditate upon these things my heart goes out in deep longing to see the truth carried in its simplicity to the homes of these people along the highways and places far removed from the crowded centers of population. We are not to wait for workers of the very highest talent to prepare the way and to show us how to labor; but, whether old or young, we have the privilege of understanding the truth as it is in Jesus, and as we see persons who are not in the possession of the comfort of God's grace, it is our privilege to visit them, and acquaint them with God's love for them and with his wonderful provision for the salvation of their souls.

In this work in the highways and the hedges, there are serious difficulties to be met and overcome. The worker, as he searches for souls, is not to fear nor be discouraged, for God is his helper, and will continue to be his helper; and he will open up ways before his servants.

We are glad, very glad, for the evidences of prosperity attending the work here at Madison. To every one assembled at this Institute, I would say: Search the Scriptures. If you do not fully realize the times in which you live, and the nearness of the end, seek to gain a fuller realization of these things by searching the Scriptures. There is a work to be done in every place. We must seek to catch the very spirit of the message.

THERE SHOULD BE SCHOOLS FOR THE COLORED PEOPLE AS WELL AS SCHOOLS IN THE HIGHLANDS

There are colored people to be saved. Yesterday it was my privilege to speak to the colored people assembled in their little church in Nashville. A goodly company of colored people listened with marked attention to the words presented.

These people did not have to do with their color. They are not accountable for the fact that they are not white; and how foolish it is for human beings that are dependent for every breath they draw to feel that we should have nothing to do with the colored people. We have a duty to perform toward them, and in the fear of God we are endeavoring to discharge this duty by providing in every possible way for them to hear the third angel's message, and to fit themselves for proclaiming the truth to their own race.

Do you know of a soul to be saved?—Christ died to save that soul, and your work is to learn how to reach the heart of that one, and point him to the Saviour.

In Acts we read the story of Philip and the nobleman—how, as an Ethiopian was journeying homeward from Jerusalem, and studying the Scriptures, Philip appeared before him, and inquired, "Understandest thou what thou readest?" The record informs us that he did not; and so Philip ascended into the chariot, and sat down by the side of the eunuch, and opened the Scriptures to his understanding, and delighted him with the truth. With enlightened heart and mind, the Ethiopian believed the message that he heard. As they journeyed on, they came to a stream of water; "and the eunuch said, See, here is water; what doth hinder me to be baptized?" Philip replied, "If thou believest with all thine heart, thou mayest." The nobleman answered, "I believe that Jesus Christ is the Son of God." Upon hearing this declaration, Philip immediately went down with the eunuch into the water, and there baptized him. Philip immediately afterward departed, as he had received a message to go to another place. The nobleman "went on his way rejoicing," a believer in the truths of God's Word.

When human hearts are susceptible to the influences of the Holy Spirit of God the Lord can do a mighty work through his servants. He can bring them into association with men and women who need help and encouragement. Everywhere we can find souls longing for the help that we might give them; and in arranging our work so as to meet this need, we must not lose sight of the neglected parts of the vineyard. Men may say that it is a waste of valuable time and money for strong young men and young women to go out into these hills and out-of-the-way places to labor. Some may contend that we cannot afford to allow young persons of talent to engage in this line of work.

"Can not afford it!" If there is but one soul to be saved, that soul is more precious than all the combined wealth of this world.

Hillcrest, a Training-School for Colored Workers

Let us thank God that the colored people have a school farm near Nashville. Day before yesterday I had the privilege of visiting the Hillcrest School, and of seeing the little houses that they have been putting up for the accommodation of a few students. A sister has recently sent them money sufficient to build a modest little cottage. In this gift the managers of the school see an evidence of God's favoring hand. The Lord is indeed moving upon the hearts of his people, and leading them to aid in the establishment of training-centers for the education of colored youth to labor among their own race. Hillcrest is a beautiful property, and gives opportunity to provide for many to receive a training for service. Let us thank God for this, and take courage.

Brother Staines and his associates are engaged in a good work. I believe that the Lord has led them, and will bless them in doing conscientiously that which they have undertaken. It is my prayer that the Lord will move upon the minds of his people to take hold of this work and help it forward. We must not let the criticism and unwise movements of some of the brethren dishearten the workers, and hinder the work. As the Lord has led Brother Staines to take up this work, so others will be led in various places to help. Men in different parts of the field as laborers together with God, will search out promising colored youth, and encourage them to attend this school. And they will help in the providing of a suitable building with class-rooms.

In past years the colored people have been terribly neglected. The time is coming when we cannot easily give them the message. Restrictions will be placed about them to such an extent that it will be next to impossible to reach them; but at the present time this is not the case, and we can go to many places where there are colored people, and can open the Scriptures to their understanding, and lead them to accept the truths of God's Word. Christ will make the impression upon their hearts.

SOME DO NOT SEE THE NEED OF RURAL SCHOOLS

There are those among us who have been in the truth for years, who have never seen nor sensed the need there is for working the highways and the hedges. All such should seek for reconversion of heart, for divine enlightenment, that they may discern the needs of a dying world. Christ came to seek and to save that which was lost. He went about on foot. He did not ride in easy conveyances. There were no railways or other modern means of travel in his day. It is known that he walked, and that multitudes joined him as he walked. Along the wayside, as he journeyed, he opened the Scriptures to the understanding of his followers. Constantly he was repeating to them the words of life. The multitudes that thronged his footsteps, were charmed with the principles brought out in his discourses.

As you go out into the highways and the hedges, let no minister of the gospel say to you, "Why do ye so?" We have for our example the ministry of Christ on this earth. We are to remove our lights from under the coverings that hide them from others, and let them shine forth amid the moral darkness.

"Ye are laborers together with God." Those who expect to wear at last a crown of life, must in this life be light-bearers.

DO NOT SAY, WE CANNOT AFFORD TO WORK IN A SELF-SUPPORTING WAY

When I first visited Madison, about five years ago, and looked over this school property, I told those who were with me, that in appearance it was similar to one of the places that had been presented before me in vision during the night season—a place where our people would have opportunity of presenting the light of truth to those who had never heard the last gospel message....

I am glad that our people are established here at Madison. I am glad to meet these workers here, who are offering themselves to go to different places. God's work is to advance steadily; his truth is to triumph. To every believer we would say: Let no one stand in the way. Say not, "We cannot afford to work in a sparsely-settled field, and largely in a self-supporting way, when out in the world are great fields where we might reach multitudes." And let none say, "We cannot afford to sustain you in an effort to work in those out-of-the-way places." What! Cannot afford it! You cannot afford not to work in these isolated places; and if you neglect such fields, the time will come when you will wish that you had afforded it. There is a world to be saved. Let some of our consecrated teachers go out into the highways and the hedges, and compel the honest in heart to come in,—not by physical force; oh, no! but with the weight of evidence as presented in God's Word.

Let no living soul—man, woman, or child—selfishly rest satisfied with a knowledge of the truth. There are honest-hearted men and women out in the hills that must be given the message of warning. There are those who cannot have the privilege of listening to the truth as it is often presented in large assemblies; these must be reached by personal effort.

There Is a Place for Everybody in the Work

We each have a work to do for God, whatever may be our occupation. Those who are on their farms, are not to think that it would be a waste of time for them to plan to go out and visit their neighbors, and hold up before them the light of the truth for this time; for even if it does seem difficult to leave the farm work, yet we shall not lose financially because of spending time in helping others. There is a God in heaven that will bless our labors. To every man—and to every woman—he has given his work. We may co-operate with Christ, by showing to others what it means to seek for eternal life as for hidden treasure. God has called upon us to do this kind of work—to look after the poor, the needy, the suffering; to be awake to the necessities of those in need of spiritual refreshment; to be ever ready to open the Scriptures to hungering souls.

DO NOT LET OTHERS DISCOURAGE YOU FROM TAKING PART IN THIS WORK

Some may say, "If I were to engage in this sort of work, some connected with the church would discountenance me." What if they should? Christ has said, "Thy righteousness shall go before thee; the glory of the Lord shall be thy rearward." We have no greater encouragement than this; we are to seek to save those who are willing to be saved. We are to bring the truth before those who will hear it. Our own souls must be filled with a love for the truth. And as we do our part faithfully, Christ will acknowledge our efforts, and add his signal blessing. And oh, what a reward awaits the winner of souls! When the gates of that beautiful city on high are swung back on their glittering hinges, and the nations that have kept the truth shall enter in, crowns of glory will be placed on their heads, and they will ascribe honor and glory and majesty to God. And at that time some will come to you, and will say, If it had not been for the words you spoke to me in kindness, if it had not been for your tears and supplications and earnest efforts, I should never have seen the King in his beauty. What a reward is this! How insignificant is the praise of human beings in this earthly, transient life, in comparison with the infinite rewards that await the faithful in the future, immortal life!

THE FARM AS A MEANS OF SUPPORT

Do you not see that the glory of the Lord is at work here at Madison? You are not to fail, not be discouraged. Bring to your house the poor that are cast out; speak to them words of comfort. I know that you are trying to do this work, and I believe that God will continue to bless you, and that he will bless this school farm.

Let us thank God for the privilege of being his light-bearers. This beautiful farm at Madison is a means of support; and it is not to hinder us from doing the very work that God has appointed us to do. And as you try to extend the influence of this school into the needy places beyond, you are doing the very work that God wants you to do. His blessing will be with every one who seeks to magnify the truth. Let not any living hand, of minister or layman, be laid upon you with the statement, "You cannot go here, you must not go there; we shall not support you if you do not go at our bidding; or if you do not give yourself to the work of bringing souls into the truth in some certain place designated by us." God will bless you as you continue to search for lost souls in out-of-the-way places.

The Reward of Those Who Work in These Hard Places

To those who are connected with our various school enterprises in the South, I would say: Let not a single hand be laid upon you to say, "You cannot do this work; you must not spend your time in this way." Time! It is God's time, and we have a right to work for the needy and the distressed, and especially for the colored people. If we continue to labor in faith and humility, God will reveal that his righteousness goes before us, and the glory of the Lord will be our rearward. As we try to follow on to know the Lord, we shall learn that his going forth is prepared as the morning. You have been gaining an understanding of this, have you not, since you have been here?

In the beginning, you did not have the bright light of day appear in all the encouraging lines; but God is working, and he will continue to work. Persevere in the humble course that you have been taking, to prepare the way for the Lord to work.

God desires that every man shall stand in his lot and in his place, and not feel as if the work was too hard. Why, he is ready to give you strength. He has granted me strength all along the way as we have journeyed eastward. He gave me strength to speak to the people as we visited place after place. At College View, Neb., I spoke on the Sabbath to two thousand people. The glory of the Lord rested upon us.

Now, my dear friends, who will be laborers together with God? Who will take up the burden of service? Who will see those that are afar off, having a hard time, and knowing nothing of the truth? Who will bring them in? Who will use their efforts to make them sons and daughters of

God? When you enter within the gates into the city, and the crown of life is placed upon your brow, and on the brows of the very ones you have worked to save, they will cast themselves upon your neck, and say, "It was you that saved my soul; I should have perished if you had not saved me from myself. You had to take a good while; but you were patient with me, and won me to a knowledge of the truth."

And then, as they lay their crowns at the feet of Jesus, and touch the golden harps that have been placed in their hands, and unite in praising and glorifying their Redeemer; and they realize that theirs is the great blessing of life, everlasting life, there will be rejoicing indeed. And oh, the thought that we may be instrumental, under God, in helping to show men and women the way of salvation, while living on this earth!

A PLEA FOR FAMILIES TO WORK IN THE SOUTH

In conclusion, I would say to every one: If you give your heart to God, if in humility you take up your appointed work, and remain faithful, at last you will hear the words, "Come, ye blessed of my Father, enter ye into the kingdom prepared for you from the foundation of the world." Is not this sufficient reward? In that happy world there will be no more temptation, no more sorrows. In your earthly life you have labored together with God; you have so lived that your righteousness has gone before you, and the glory of the Lord has been your rearward.

Oh, let us work today, while we still have opportunity! Let us strive to bring souls into the light of truth, by opening to them the Scriptures, and by praying with them, and urging them to accept Jesus as their Saviour. And as you engage in this work, Jesus is your Helper, even the same Jesus that has passed over the road before us, and has given his life in our behalf. If we make sacrifices on the right hand and on the left; if we seek to be laborers together with God,—without whom we can do nothing aright,—we shall at last have the life that measures with the everlasting life of God—no prospect of falling, no Satan to tempt and lead astray, no death. I long to see families engaged in soul-winning—seeking to let their light shine amid the moral darkness of the world. May God help us, is my prayer.

Recent Instruction Concerning Schools in the South

Subjects to be Taught in These Schools

There is constant danger among our people that those who engage in labor in our schools and sanitariums will entertain the idea that they must get in line with the world, study the things which the world studies, and become familiar with the things that the world becomes familiar with. This is one of the greatest mistakes that could be made. We shall make grave mistakes unless we give special attention to the searching of the Word....

Strong temptations will come to many who place their children in our schools because they desire the youth to secure what the world regards as the most essential education. Who knows what the most essential education is unless it is the education to be attained from that Book which is the foundation of all true knowledge. Those who regard as essential the knowledge to be gained along the line of worldly education, are making a great mistake,—one which will cause them to be swayed by individual opinions that are human and erring. To those who feel that their children must have what the world calls the essential education, I would say, Bring your children to the simplicity of the Word of God, and they will be safe. We are going to be greatly scattered before long and what we do must be done quickly.

The light has been given me that tremendous pressure will be brought upon every Seventh-day Adventist with whom the world can get into close connection. We need to understand these things. Those who seek the education that the world esteems so highly, are gradually drifting farther and farther from the principles of truth until they become educated worldlings. At what price have, they gained their education! They have parted with the Holy Spirit of God. They have chosen to accept what the world calls knowledge in the place of the truths which God has committed to men through his ministers and prophets and apostles. And there are some who, having secured this worldly education, think that they can introduce it into our schools. But let me tell you that you must not take what the world calls the higher education and bring it into our schools and sanitariums and churches. I speak to you definitely. This must not be done....

If we will look to him, the Lord will help us to understand what constitutes true higher education. It is not to be gained by putting yourself through a long course of continual study. In such a course you will get some things that are valuable, and many things that are not. The Lord would have us become laborers together with him. He is our helper. He would have us come close to him and learn of him with all humility of mind.... Do not regard as most essential the theoretical education.—*Instruction to Students and Teachers of Union College*, May, 1909.

The presentation in our schools should not now be as it has been in the past in introducing many things as essential that are only of minor importance. The light given me is that the commandments of God, the will of the Lord regarding each individual, should be made the chief study of every student who would be fitted for the higher grades of the school above—Private *Letter*, January, 1909.

WORK FOR TRUE HIGHER EDUCATION

Now is our time to work. The end of all things is at hand.... By pen and voice labor to sweep back the false ideas that have taken possession of men's minds regarding the higher education.—Personal Letter, June, 1909.

I do not say that there should be no study of the languages. The languages should be studied. Before long there will be a positive necessity for many to leave their homes and work among those of other languages; and those who have some knowledge of foreign languages will thereby be able to communicate with those who know not the truth. Some of our people will learn the languages in the countries to which they are sent. This is the better way. And there is One, who will stand right by the side of a faithful worker to open the understanding and to give wisdom. If you did not know a word of the foreign languages, the Lord could make your work fruitful.—*Instruction to Students and Teachers of Union College*, May, 1909.

Mission Schools Should be Started for They Will Hasten the End

Every possible means should be devised to establish schools of the Madison order in various parts of the South; and those who lend their means and their influence to help this work, are aiding the cause of God. I am instructed to say to those who have means to spare: Help the work at Madison. You have no time to lose. Satan will soon rise up to create hindrances; let the work go forward while it may. Let us strengthen this company of educators to continue the good work in which they are engaged, and labor to engage others to do a similar work. Then the light of truth will be carried in a simple and effective way, and a great work will be accomplished for the Master in a short time.—"An Appeal for the Madison School."

Enter the Highways and Byways

The light is given that we must not have special anxiety to crowd too many interests into one locality, but should look for places in out-of-the-way districts.... The seeds of truth are to be sown in uncultivated centers....

While such great expense is incurred to enlighten the people of foreign tongues we are all to be just as wide awake to reach, if possible, the foreigners and the unconverted in our own land.... There is missionary work to be done in many unpromising places. The missionary spirit needs to take hold of our souls, inspiring us to reach classes for whom we had not planned to labor, and ways and places that we had no idea of working.—Personal *Letter*, October, 1908.

Where are the Workers for These Needy Places

The church-members should be drawn out to labor.... I am instructed to say that the angels of God will direct in the opening of fields nigh as well as afar off.... God calls upon believers to obtain an experience in missionary work by branching out into new territory, and working intelligently for the people in the byways.... The Lord is certainly opening the way for us as a people to divide and subdivide the companies that have been growing too large to work together to the greatest advantage.—Personal *Letter*, October, 1908.

HOW TO START WORK IN THE SOUTH

Properties will be offered for sale in the rural districts at a price below the real cost, because the owners desire city advantages, and it is these rural locations that we desire to obtain for our schools.—Personal *Letter*.

CONCERNING THE SOUTHERN WORK

Extracts from Talks Given by Mrs. E. G. White at the General Conference Meeting, Washington, D.C., May 1909.

HIGHLAND SCHOOLS AS EVANGELIZING AGENCIES

On my journey to Washington I had some experience in going not only to the highways, but also to the hedges. I saw something of the work that is being done in the mission schools near Nashville. Little companies of workers are going out into the mountains and laboring for those who have not heard the message, and here and there little companies of believers are being raised up. Who would dare to put their hand on such workers and say, You must not labor thus; it costs too much. Can it compare with the sacrifice that Christ made in order to save perishing souls? My brethren and sisters, I ask you in the name of Jesus of Nazareth to take your light from under the bushel, and let it shine forth that others may be profited.—*The General Conference Bulletin*, May 17, 1909.

GIVE THE SCHOOLS LIBERTY TO CARRY OUT GOD'S PLANS

There are our schools. They are to be conducted in such a way that they will develop missionaries who will go out to the highways and hedges to sow seeds of truth. This was the commission of Christ to his followers....

Do not allow any man to come in as an arbitrary ruler, and say, You must not go here, and you must not go there; you must do this and you must not do that. We have a great and important work to do, and God would have us take hold of that work intelligently. The placing of men in positions of responsibility in various conferences, does not make them gods. No one has sufficient wisdom to act without counsel. Men need to consult with their brethren, to counsel together, to pray together, and to plan together for the advancement of the work. Let laborers kneel down together and pray to God, asking him to direct their course. There has been a great lack with us on this point. We have trusted too much to men's devisings. We cannot afford to do this. Perilous times are upon us, and we must come to the place where we know that the Lord lives and rules, and that he dwells in the hearts of the children of men. We must have confidence in God....

There are schools to be established in foreign countries and in our own country. We must learn from God how to manage these schools. They are not to be conducted as many of them have been conducted. Our institutions are to be regarded as God's instrumentalities for the furtherance of his work in the earth. We must look to God for guidance and wisdom; we must plead with him to teach us how to carry the work solidly. Let us recognize the Lord as our teacher and guide, and then we shall carry the work in correct lines....

In all our schools we need to have a correct understanding of what the essential education is. Men talk much of higher education, but who can define what the higher education is? The highest education is found in the Word of the living God. That education which teaches us to submit our souls to God in all humility, and which enables us to take the Word of God and believe just what it says, is the education that is most needed....

If men will not move in concert in the great and grand work for this time, there will be confusion. It is not a good sign when men refuse to unite with their brethren, and prefer to act alone.... On the other hand, the leaders among God's people are to guard against the danger of condemning the methods of individual workers who are led by the Lord to do a special work that but few are fitted to do. Let brethren in responsibility be slow to criticize the movements that are not in perfect harmony with their methods of labor. Let them never suppose that every plan should reflect their own personality. Let them not fear to trust another's methods; for by withholding their confidence from a fellow brother laborer who, with humility and consecrated zeal, is doing a special work in God's appointed way, they are retarding the advancement of the Lord's cause.... God can and will use those who have not a thorough education in the schools of men. A doubt of his power to do this is manifest unbelief.

There are hundreds of our people who ought to be out in the field who are doing little or nothing for the advancement of the message.—*The General Conference Bulletin*, May 31, 1909.

THE EDUCATION TO BE OFFERED IN OUR SCHOOLS

There are many who believe that in order to be fitted for acceptable service, they must go through a long course of study under learned teachers in some school of the world. This they must do, it is true, if they desire to secure what the world calls essential knowledge. But we do not say to our youth, You must study, study, keeping your mind all the time on books. Nor do we say to them, You must spend all the time in acquiring the so-called higher education. Let us ask, What is the object of true higher education? Is it not that we may stand in right relation to God? The test of all education should be, Is it fitting us to keep our minds fixed upon the mark of the prize of the high calling of God in Christ Jesus?—*The General Conference Bulletin*, May 30, 1909.

MANUAL TRAINING A NECESSARY PART OF EVERY CURRICULUM

Our youth should be taught from their very childhood how to exercise the body and the mind proportionately. It is not wise to send the children to schools where they are subject to long hours of confinement, and where they will gain no knowledge of what healthful living means. Place them under the tuition of those who respect the body and treat it with consideration. Do not place your children in an unfavorable position, where they cannot receive the training that will enable them to bear test and trial....

Students need not talk of their attainments in the so-called higher education if they have not learned to eat and drink to the glory of God, and to exercise brain, bone, and muscle in such a way as to prepare for the highest possible service. The whole being must be brought into exercise if we would secure a healthy condition of mind; the mental and the physical powers should be used proportionately....

To those who are desirous of being efficient laborers in God's cause, I would say, if you are putting an undue weight of labor on the brain, thinking you will lose ground unless you study all the time, you had better change your views and your course of action. Unless greater care is exercised in this respect, there are many who will go down to the grave prematurely. This you cannot afford to do; for there is a world to be saved.... Everywhere, everywhere the truth is to stand forth in its glorious power and in its simplicity. Do not boast of what you know, but take your case to God. Say to him, I comply with the conditions.—*The General Conference Bulletin*, May 30, 1909.

POINTED SENTENCES FROM OLDER TESTIMONIES

"In the future, men in the common walks of life will be impressed by the Spirit of the Lord to leave their ordinary employment, and go forth to proclaim the last message of mercy. As rapidly as possible they are to be prepared for labor, that success may crown their efforts."

"In the South there is much that could be done by lay-members of the church, persons of limited education. There are men, women and children who need to be taught to read."

"Shall not the number of missionaries to the South be multiplied? Shall we not hear of many volunteers who are ready to enter this field?"

"The whole church needs to be imbued with the missionary spirit; then there will be many to work unselfishly in various ways as they can, without being salaried."

"We need schools that will be self-supporting, and this can be if teachers will be helpful, industrious, and economical."

"Schools are to be established away from the cities, where the youth can learn to cultivate the soil, and thus help to make themselves and the school self-supporting.... Let means be gathered for the establishment of such schools."

"There is to be a work done in the South, and it needs men and women who will not need to be preachers so much as teachers,—humble men who are not afraid to work as farmers to educate the Southerners how to till the soil, for whites and blacks need to be educated in this line."

"There are lessons of the highest importance to be learned from the Word of God. This great Book is open to us that our youth may be educated after the manner of the sons of the prophets. We, as a people, should carry on the work of the education of our youth in such a way that they will be guarded against living self-indulgent lives."

"I have been shown that in our educational work we are not to follow the methods that have been adopted in our older established schools. There is among us too much clinging to old customs, and because of this we are far behind where we should be in the development of the third angel's message."

"Years have passed into eternity with small results that might have shown the accomplishment of a great work."

"The usefulness learned on the school farm is the very education that is most essential for those who go out as missionaries to many foreign fields."

"There has been a decided failure to meet the requirements of God in the Southern field. We need to ask the Lord to give us understanding that we may see our lack, and take in the situation in the South, and the need of doing the missionary work that lies right at hand."

"For twenty years it has been before our people that they must do a special work in the Southern States. When the Lord repeatedly sends messages to his people, it is because he desires them to follow the light he gives."

"We are not to work in the same place over and over again, leaving many places where the last message of warning has not yet been proclaimed.... Memphis, New Orleans, and other cities of the South are calling for workers filled with the power of the Spirit."

"As a people we need yet to learn what it means to fill our places as missionaries among a people who know not the truth for this time."

"I have received words of encouragement for our workers at Madison, who are trying to give their students a practical education while establishing them in the principles of our faith. The students are learning how to till the soil, and how to build plain, simple houses. And these students are encouraged to go out and establish other industrial schools where they, in turn, can educate their students how to plan and how to build."

APPENDIX E — LETTER OF A. W. SPALDING

Copy of Letter from A. W. Spalding to L. K. Dickson,
General Conference of Seventh-day Adventists
May, 1953

Dear Brother Dickson:

You may sometime find the leisure and inclination to read this letter. It is with the deepest sympathy and desire to cooperate that I greet the coming of you brethren—you, Professor Cossentine, and Elder Bradley—to Southern Missionary College, with the avowed purpose of consulting with the faculty over the broad problems of Christian Education. Your few words with me after your initial talk, as well as your public utterances, reveal the consciousness of deep wound in our educational body, the heart of all our cause, and of the necessity of a radical cure if a solution is to be found.

The faculty are invited to discuss with you freely the causes of the malady, the effects of which are seen in spiritual lethargy, false and injurious attitudes, and lack of power to finish God's work. I have contemplated entering into the public discussion; but if I should speak out my heart in surveying the causes and suggesting the remedy, it would take an unconscionable length of time, and moreover would, as I reflect, be impolitic and unwise. It would run counter to typical lines of thinking among our educators, and if it were received as having any value and weight, would tend at this juncture to confuse students and perhaps teachers, and would arouse controversy. The area of reform, as I conceive it, goes so deep into our philosophy and practice as to point to complete revolution in our denominational policies of education, a revolution made necessary because we have previously revolved so far to the left that our backs are turned upon our pattern.

I have no conceit of being the instructor of our leaders, of whose ability and sincerity (speaking generally) I have no doubt. I am but a little one in our ranks, without the prestige and the learning that would qualify a counselor of weight. Yet my mind is so burdened with the state of our educational work that when I tell myself to keep silence and divorce myself from all sense of responsibility, I cannot rest or sleep. And this letter is begun at midnight because of that fact.

I have had the privilege of long connection with and experience in our educational work, both in and out of our schools; and I have through all this half century and more been a student of the educational principles and structure and processes which God has given us through the instrumentality of Ellen G. White. I have perceived in her writings not merely aphoristic maxims to grace dissertations on religion and learning; but rather a deeply conceived, well integrated system of education, embracing philosophy, range, form, content, method, and above all spirit. These writings constitute a blueprint which, also, our history shows has been little read, less understood, not at all comprehended. Our departure from it has been a consequence of this lack of perception and will to follow. The best compendium of this wealth of educational wisdom is the book, *Education*. It is supplemented by various other works, such as *Counsels to Teachers*, *Fundamentals of Christian Education*, *The Ministry of Healing*, and various other works on particular phases, including especially the educational department in *Testimonies*, Vol. 6.

I am therefore moved to record briefly my convictions of the deep-seated causes of the spiritual poverty and confusion among our workers and our people, stemming chiefly from our schools. Being advanced in years, I may not live to see even the beginning of the reform; for if it comes—and come it must before this people is ready to meet the Lord Jesus—it involves so radical and consummate an overturning that, except in the inscrutable miracles of God, it cannot be accomplished in a day. But I desire to leave to my children at least and to whomever will heed, a testament of my faith and vision.

No reform can be adequate and effective except as it goes to the root of the malady. Little doses and patches of remedies, treating symptoms and scratches, are as inadequate and futile as they are blind. They are but healing "the hurt of the daughter of my people slightly." The fruit of the Tree of Knowledge of Good and Evil is not destroyed by rejecting one or a few wormy specimens. The tree must be rejected; we must turn to the Tree of Life. For brevity's sake, in the points I make following, I cite as authority only one directive from the Spirit of Prophecy; in most cases there is abundance of testimony besides.

Twenty-five years ago, in 1928, we came to our educational Kadesh-barnea. The Promised Land was before us, but the majority of our spies brought back an evil report. Discouraged at the report of the giants and the walled cities, we turned away from the commands of the Lord, and rejected His instructions not to seek our education in the universities, the schools of the world. (*Fundamentals of Christian Education*, 347, 359, 451, 567-474). The true higher education lies in the study of God's revealed knowledge and wisdom. Ibid; Education 14. There were a few Calebs and Joshuas there, but their voices were drowned by the clamors of the multitude. We voted for affiliation and accreditation, with all that it involved of affinity with the world's education.

The result of a generation of training in postgraduate work in the schools of the world is the molding of our educational institutions and curricula after the pattern there set before us or, if not there born, at least strengthened. If we had instead turned to an intensive study and faithful following of the Spirit of Prophecy, with our minds enlightened by the Holy Spirit, we would now be so far ahead of the world in our ideals and demonstrations, that we should be the head, not the tail, walking in chains in the train or our captors. If that characterization seems unjustified, if they cannot see it for a fact, let me ask, what can be expected when we turn our backs upon God's directions? Are they inconsequential? Can they be explained away? Do we suffer no retribution for our disregard and disobedience? So reasoned Israel through its tortuous history of disloyalty and idolatry, till, as the Chronicler says, "there was no remedy."

I have been challenged by some officials to tell how we can meet the difficulties, the legal obstructions to our operation as individuals or institutions, without conforming to the regulations of the accrediting agencies and the laws of the states, and therefore to the education afforded by the universities. I do not know; no man knows. But when Israel came up to the Red Sea and to the Jordan in its flood, no man-made devices, no counsels of the worldly-wise, could save them from the Egyptians or enable them to enter the Promised Land. And this I know from my study of the Testimonies on education, that the blueprint of the Christian education given us sets forth the truest, the most serviceable, the wisest, the grandest system of education ever proposed, so far superior to the systems of the world as to outshine them as the sun outshines the candle. If this seems extravagant, it is only to those whom the candle has enthralled and who have not seen the light of the sun.

To many it seems ridiculous to charge our schools with fault in curriculum or method. They point to the improvements and supposed improvements, in libraries, laboratories, techniques, and affiliations, and to the more scientific methods in teaching, which are or which seem to be the fruit of cooperation with the world. Would we counsel a return to the innocent days of Mary Hopkins on one end of a log and a student on the other? Would we reduce our faculties of masters and doctors to the status of unschooled teachers like Uriah Smith, Stephen Haskell, and Goodloe Bell? It does not follow that taking heed to the Testimonies would reduce our teaching bodies to the state of ignoramuses and imbeciles. And the men who were scorned because they had no degree were yet men of wisdom and skill and ability. G. H. Bell, though he had no scholastic degree, was the one man in these early times who perceived the vision vouchsafed by the Lord to His unschooled servant, Ellen G. White, and who sought with all his ingenuity and power to put the principles into operation. He was rejected as leader in favor of a university-trained man who later in life confessed to me that he had then been, in his own words, "an educated fool." And the culmination of the policy gave us an Alexander McLearn, who put Battle Creek College out of operation for a whole year. We learn little, and we learn slowly.

Who can read, with mind enlightened by the Holy Spirit, that central masterpiece of Sister White's, the book Education, and not perceive the deep wisdom, the all-embracing science of the education God has offered to us? We have never really studied, nor practiced, nor sought to attain what that book teaches. To those who could have been instructed and enlightened by study of the Testimonies, there would have been no need of the spur of accrediting associations or statute laws to inspire improvement of our facilities and methods. We were asleep, but we needed no wine of Babylon to inflame us; we need the fruit of the Tree of Life.

The closer affinity we make with the schools of the world, the farther we depart from the presence of God. To read the first article in *Testimonies for the Church*, Vol. 6, in the section, "Education," "The Need of Educational Reform," is to feel a dagger struck into our educational policies. Are we receiving the mark of the beast and his image, or the seal of God? Page 130.

Yet our schools are infinitely better than the schools of the world. They are "cities of refuge" for our youth. The principles of our faith have had much effect upon our lives and our policies. Slighted and neglected though they have been in great degree, yet their impact upon our lives has been considerable. In our schools there are observed and inculcated correct principles of social behaviour, diet and health, avoidance of narcotics, studiousness, reverence and devotion which have greater or less effect upon the students.

And the high moral character of our teachers in general, their varying degrees of devotion and consecration, their perception of spiritual values, have a most telling effect upon students. Would that it were greater, but thank God for what it is. Many teachers who have taken their post-graduate work in schools of the world yet number among them men of deep piety and whole-souled consecration. They may be Moseses needing only the wilderness experience.

Nevertheless there is not perfection. The little elevation above the world to which we have attained, morally, is not the high mark set before us by God. Even in the days of Ahab, the impact of the diluted worship of Jehovah had such an effect upon the rulers that their reputation in the world was high: "The kings of Israel are merciful kings." But that did not make Ahab a man of God, nor remove Jezebel's influence. Elijah and Elisha have yet a work to do for us.

"We need now to begin over again. Reforms must be entered into with heart, and soul, and will. …If there is not in some respects an education of an altogether different character from that which has been carried on in some of our schools, we need not have gone to the expense of purchasing lands and erecting school-buildings." (*Testimonies for the Church*, Vol. 6, p. 142). I was a student in Battle Creek College at the time that was written; I am a teacher now. My scholastic life spans the years; and I testify that the need of reforms is greater now than it was then. For we have retrograded. We say we are different from the world's schools—because we teach the Bible. But other church schools teach Bible too; the question is, How true is the Teaching? Minds that turn from the light of God in any phase or any respect are dim in perception of the spirit of Bible truth. The truth of God goes deeper than a creed. Doctrine is the framework of truth, but without the life it becomes a stark skeleton.

But so subtle is the influence which has made us depart from the divine blueprint that it is imperceptible to those involved, and like Malachi's people, they ask in injured innocence: "Wherein have we departed from the blueprint? Give us specific instances."

I will cite five areas of disharmony with the word of God in educational theories and practices in our schools. They are only a few examples of disobedience; there are others, as for instance, the social structure and code, agriculture as the ABC of educational effort; industries, ostentation in place of simplicity, the character of entertainment, preoccupation with things of the flesh and the world. If all our variances from the blueprint are not the product of participation with the world, they are in any case fostered by contact with and participation in the ideals and methods received in the world's schools. Ahaz did not need to go to Damascus to prove his disloyalty; but when he went, he brought back the heathen altar and put it in the house of God. I will now list the five transgressions:

1. Incentive, motivation. In our first meeting here, discussion turned for a time upon unlovely and even scandalous self-urge of workers to be recognized as great men, to covet position and authority, to engage in rivalry for honor and lordship. The question was timidly raised whether the school policy of clothing students with responsibility and bestowing honors and emolument upon them was responsible for inculcating this spirit. The problem goes much deeper than that. Developing youth need to be judiciously accorded increasing responsibility; but what is the incentive offered to work and organize and improve?—that is the determining factor in whether that social and managerial education is beneficial or injurious.

The world's chief incentive is competition, rivalry. I could write a treatise upon the nature and ramifications of this selfish urge; that I have done in my book, *Who Is the Greatest?* It deserves study. Both the Bible and the Spirit of Prophecy condemn rivalry (and competition, its genesis) as the motivation of the Christian. Mark 10:42-45. (*Education*, pp. 225, 226).

The Christian incentive is unselfish love, the love of Christ, cooperation, ministry. We acknowledge this, but we mingle with, and often let become dominant the incentive of competition. We honor the temple and offer sacrifices there, because it is beautiful and gives us prestige; but we keep the high places also, and bow down before the images of Baal and Astarte. In what? In our class incentives, with marks and gradings and prizes and special honors, in our social life, in our recreations, and ultimately in the professional life of our students when they leave school and enter the work of God. We stage contests and give rewards and prizes for the winners. And this is so common and time honored a practice that we stare in amazement if it is challenged. To the end of Israel and Judah, save for the spasmodic reforms of Josiah, the high places remained and were considered to be, in a degree, a part of the worship of Jehovah. We are repeating the history. But the incentive and the worship place of the Christian is not competition, rivalry, but the pure urge of love, the love of God.

Adoption of the Christian incentive of love, when it is studied in all its aspects and applications, would revolutionize our system and our lives, and produce men and women who know the spirit of Christ, who buried Himself in the furrow of the world's need, that He might bring forth more fruit. Until the policy and practice of our schools is reversed, we shall continue to turn out self-centered, egotistic, arrogant young workers. There will, of course, be exceptions, in the degree that the love of God works secretly in the life of this and that young man and woman. But what is the responsibility of the school? The spirit of rivalry may begin in the home, it certainly exists in the community which helps to mold the early character, it may be and usually is in the church; but our schools instead of correcting it, foster it. The college is the last opportunity for reform; and the college is not performing its function.

2. **Literature.** Despite clear and explicit instruction in the *Testimonies* (*Education*, pp. 226, 227), a great volume indeed of instruction upon the evil of subjecting our students to the influence of pagan authors, our courses in literature continue to present such writers and to enforce their study. Some teachers of English seem unable to distinguish between the good and the evil in literature, except the extremes. From Homer to Shakespeare and such modern pygmies as Walt Whitman, they induct their students into pagan and neo-pagan masses of crime, blood, obscenity, and blasphemy. That there are cases of beauty and probity in all these authors is true; the Devil clothes his progeny in purple and gold. But the waters of purity are fouled in puddles of mud. Our study of literature should be selective, as professor Bell demonstrated, and not comprehensive, as all worldly concepts of the study of literature dictate. Our objective in education must be, not to reach the level and copy the ways of the schools of the world; but rather to adjudge the needs of the church in its particular work. What Christian education aims at is character building; what the church and the world need is "young men and young women … fit to stand at the head of their families. But such an education is not to be acquired by the study of heathen classics." (*Ministry of Healing*, p. 444).

The laws of the accrediting associations may be given as an excuse for continuing this transgression of the divine will. How pitiful the excuse in the eyes of God and in view of the characters being formed in our youth. But as I discovered when teaching literature, those laws are not so inflexible. Unless teachers have acquired an appetite for the fleshpots of Egypt, they are not bound by any rigid laws to feed from them. The teaching of such classic filth and evil, perverse-ly, defeats its own objective, by lowering the taste of students and leading them to indulge in the poorest types of fiction and sports news and comics. By such means, even the teaching of Biblical literature as a school study is rendered distasteful, and along with uninspired teaching adds to the aversion of students for the Scriptures. What are we doing to our prospective ministers and teachers?

3. Recreation. The instruction of the Spirit of Prophecy upon recreation is constructive and not merely negative. *Education*, pp. 207-222. But it is sufficiently explicit in condemning competitive sports to be definitive in this field; and all the fallacious reasoning the "change of venue," falls so short of conviction that, in the end, there comes to be only the bold and open-faced defiance of the instruction, as being unrealistic and oppressive. *Counsels to Teachers*, p. 350 ff. There was a time, forty to fifty years ago, when competitive sports were banished from nearly all, if not all of our colleges. But they have come back with force, and their adoption is increasing. Teachers seem unable to meet, constructively or even defensively, the headlong demand of students for sports. And the reason again is that we have failed to study and follow and develop the instruction of the Testimonies of God's Spirit.

There is such an inspiration, such a healthy recreation, combined with science and growing appreciation, in the study of nature and in its activities, from hiking to gardening, such a wealth of wisdom, the wisdom of God's word, to be garnered from its use, as far outstrips the trivial and debasing rewards of sports. On the other hand, there is no greater ally of the evil incentive of rivalry than the competitive sports. And this stronghold of the devil is one of the hardest to take. I do not believe in harshly removing sports from the life of the school, without substituting true recreation in their place. And this cannot be done suddenly and arbitrarily. The substitution must be a growth, not a displacement. There should be built up such an experience, such a delight and enthusiasm for the things of God's creation as would displace naturally the urge in rivalry in athletic games. This is a tremendous task and opportunity for our teachers and our schools. Unless it is realized, we shall forever be hanging on the precipice of disloyalty and loss.

4. Nature study and occupation. There are many studies foisted upon our students which are relatively unimportant, and which crowd the program so tightly as to forbid the inclusion of neglected but more important studies. I cite nature study as an example. God has three books: the Bible, nature and history. He made the creation to be His first book, to convey to us His thoughts. Later, because of sin, He gave the Bible, which illumines and interprets both nature and history. The study of nature—not merely to know its mechanism, but to explore God's thoughts—is a vital part of Christian education, and this the Testimonies reveal and emphasize. But who among us is able to read and to teach the word of God from nature? The opening direction of the Three Angels' Messages, our text, is ignored; for we cannot know the God who created unless we know His creation.

The natural sciences are, generally speaking, taught as dry skeletonized subjects—names, orders, laws, classifications; and to many students who take them as an aid in getting their degrees, they are an utter bore. This is not opening the works of God to students. Nor can the science of reading God's word be gotten in the schools of the world. It can only be obtained through combination of the study of nature, Bible, and Testimonies. This is not to ignore the findings of science and the vast store of knowledge which, admittedly, are to be found in the schools of the world and the teachers in them, as well as of scientists and savants outside the school. But this knowledge can be gained without … our actual enrollment in them; and such knowledge is to be screened through the truths revealed to us by God himself. If any men are to be trusted to the clutch of the universities, they should be carefully selected men, not an indiscriminate mob of youth intent upon grabbing higher degrees; and we must realize that even in making such selections and recommendations, we are running the risk of sacrificing some portion of our precious heritage.

But we are not including the study of God's creation in any adequate or perspicacious way in our colleges. (I except certain cases, where men of learning and consecration have made shining marks as true teachers.) Recently a theological student, bright and enterprising, asked me, "How do you find God's word in nature? I go outdoors and sit in the midst of things; I see, but I do not get any heavenly message. How do you learn to read God's thoughts in nature?"

I said: "A good way to start is to follow the counsel on page 120 of *Education* to compare Bible with nature."

"Why I didn't know there was anything in *Education* about nature," he said.

"Have you read the book?"

"Yes, three times, once in a course. But I don't remember there is anything about nature in it."!!!

We have located our college in the midst of God's beautiful handiwork, but the eyes and ears of our students are kept so grindingly on their scholastic tasks and extracurricular duties, and there is such a paucity of invigorating leadership in the things of God revealed in nature, that not one in ten students has either a knowledge of or an interest in nature study. Yet, "On the lily's petals God has written a message for you—written in language that your heart can read only as it unlearns the lessons of distrust and selfishness and corroding care." (*Thoughts from the Mount of Blessing*, p. 109 [old edition, p. 143]).

5. Parent Education. We started our educational edifice at the top, with a college. We were nearly a quarter of a century late in instituting elementary education. We have never applied ourselves to laying the foundation, the pre-school education of the child. Yet all this is laid out for us in the Testimonies, and it is told us that the early years are the most determinative in the education of the individual. *Counsels to Teachers*, p. 107. The earliest counsels on education were devoted to the home life and the training which parents should give their children. (*Testimonies for the Church*, Vol. 3, p. 131, ff.) Very specific outlines of instruction were laid out, and the instruction, (far anticipatory of scientific findings) was given that until a child is eight or ten years of age, his only school should be the home and his only teachers the parents. (*Counsels to Teachers*, pp. 79, 80, 107). But this presupposes the competency of the parents as teachers. (*Id.*, p. 108). Fatuously, disingenuously, perversely, this statement has been taken by many educators and administrators to excuse them from any participation in this program: "Let the parents do it."

But parents have received no training from the church's schools for their assumption of the role as teachers. What knowledge and ability any of them may have has been inherited from their parents or picked up by casual reading or chance instruction. Seldom is this most important branch of study organized, integrated, complete. The church in its educational system has had no place for this. Yet the church is directed to give that education to parents. (*Education*, pp. 275, 276). There should be instruction given to all students in college, and probably in the academy, in the duties, privileges, and responsibilities of home life and parenthood. (*Ministry of Healing*, p. 444).

The deplorable state of our Seventh-day Adventist homes—not, doubtless averaging worse than the homes of the world, yet not superior in general and in numberless instances most sickening—is attributable to the gross neglect of the church's educational program. Not only should students be trained for marriage and parenthood, but teachers especially training for the teaching of parents and the instituting of demonstration preschools, should be prepared to go into our churches whether old or new, and likewise into non-Adventist communities, and give a thorough Christian training to parents and children. Especially should this instruction be given to our prospective ministers and their wives.

Yet our college boards shrink from and choose to ignore this basic need. Intent upon economics, their minds falter before the assumed and probable cost. There is money for magnificent buildings of science, for ornate temples of worship, for everything but the foundation work of education, the training of parents for the preschool education of their children.

Seventeen years after she had effected the institution of the elementary church school work, Sister White said to me of the training of parents: "This is the most important work before us as a people and we have not begun to touch it with the tips of our fingers." Forty years ago and we have not even yet begun to touch it with the tips of our fingers. How shall we lift the level of piety and power in the church while we neglect the very foundation of our educational work? "If the foundations be destroyed, what shall the righteous do?"

Even this world is rapidly forging ahead of us, of us who had the light and instruction seventy-five years ago. We are at the tag end of educational progress, when we should be at the head. Schools of the world, from high schools to universities, are formulating policies and instituting means for education in home life and training. We cannot depend upon the universities and teachers' colleges to give our teachers this training. While we may gather from their findings and experience much of value to us, we cannot afford to subject our preschool teachers to their classes; for so much of error is mingled with the truth. All that we get from them, by reading and by consultation, must be screened through the sacred instruction given us by God. When will our authorities awake to the vital and pressing necessity and act? (*Testimonies for the Church*, Vol 6, p. 196).

Never, for all our alarms and challenges and calls to repentance and prayer and revival efforts, never shall we effect a reform, till we go to the roots of the matter, face up as Christian men to the stark facts, repent of our folly and indifference and neglect, and turn with all our heart to God whose work we are expected to finish in this generation. Joshua 7:10-13.

May the Lord so direct and control us that our colleges shall become more like God's schools of the prophets than like Rome's College of the Propaganda. Here lies our only hope of being the instrument in God's hands to finish His work, rather than being rejected and cast off as were His chosen people the Jews.

Sincerely,

A. W. Spalding

Adventist Pioneer Library

For more information, visit:
www.APLib.org

or write to:
apl@netbox.com

CPSIA information can be obtained
at www.ICGtesting.com
Printed in the USA
LVHW05s1948200618
581389LV00015B/232/P